# PHOTOGRAPHING YOUR ARTWORK

# PHOTOGRAPHING YOUR ARTWORK

RUSSELL HART

North Light Books
Cincinnati, Ohio

Published by North Light Books, an imprint of F&W Publications, Inc., 1507 Dana Ave., Cincinnati, Ohio 45207.

93 92 91 90 89        6 5 4 3

Manufactured in U.S.A.

**Library of Congress Cataloging-in-Publication Data**

Hart, Russell, 1953-
  Photographing your artwork.

  Includes index.
  1. Photography of art. I. Title.
TR657.H37   1987      778.9'97      87-5685
ISBN 0-89134-187-0

*Design by Clare Finney*

*Illustrated by Nan Starr*

*To my parents, for all the nights of running water.*

## ACKNOWLEDGMENTS

*This book would never have happened if not for the desperate need expressed by artist-friends for such a resource. My thanks to all of them, including those not listed here. I hope they never have to hire another photographer.*

*A number of artists let me photograph their work for this book. Many others offered, or let me use slides I'd already made of their artwork. They include Susan Jane Belton, Charles Crowley, Diefo, Celie Fago, Ralph Helmick, Susan Mampre, Martha Maness, Joyce McDaniels, Susan Morrison, John Neprud, Pina, Hope Ricciardi, and last but not least, Dan Wills. Rob and Holly Emslie lent me my own work and put up with a bare spot for months. They weren't alone.*

*I'm grateful also to the deans of the School of the Museum of Fine Arts, Boston, especially to Gene Ward, for whom a number of the photographs in the book were originally taken, and who lent me the slides. Jim Field, director of the Museum School Gallery, gave advice and let the gallery be used for installation photographs.*

*Special thanks to Wayne Lemmon, former head of the photography studio at the Boston Museum of Fine Arts, a superb photographer who took a chance on me in spite of my "fine art" portfolio and taught me most of what I know about photographing artwork; to John Woolf and Tom Lang, who understand this stuff much better than I do; and to the rest of the folks in the Museum of Fine Arts Photography Department.*

*I owe a further debt of gratitude to Henry Horenstein, whose wisdom and experience have been invaluable in this and many other projects; to Dorothea Boniello, formerly of the Massachusetts Artists Foundation, whose early interest in the project encouraged me; to Nan Starr, whose illustrations keep technical material understandable and lively; and again to John Woolf, who read the manuscript and took pictures for me when I didn't have the time. Thanks also to David Lewis, editor of North Light Books, who saw the merits of the project when others didn't, and to Greg Albert, my editor, whose understanding of artists' needs helped shape the book.*

*Most of all, thanks and love to my parents, who let me turn a good part of their house into a studio when I was short of space, and to my wife, Rena, who loved me in spite of the craziness that such a project inevitably causes.*

# CONTENTS

# INTRODUCTION

A good photograph of an artwork is almost always a revelation to the artist. Quite literally, it casts the work in a new light: with even illumination, a painting's rich color and detail are revealed after months of hiding in the chiaroscuro of a painter's loft; against a seamless background, the elegant lines of a sculpture are finally freed from the clutter of a dusty studio. Photographing your artwork carefully might be worth the trouble simply for this kind of fresh perspective on it. But there are more compelling reasons.

## WHY YOU NEED GOOD PHOTOGRAPHS OF YOUR WORK

If you've ever looked into showing and selling your artwork, you know that most art galleries, museums, and other exhibition facilities routinely ask to see slides before they'll look at the real thing. Agencies that administer arts programs also do their initial screening with slide submissions. Galleries keep slide files of work by artists they represent or exhibit, to show prospective buyers examples of work that can't be kept in the gallery itself, often because it is too large or cumbersome. And certainly, if you sell or make a gift of an artwork, you'll want a good photograph of it for your own records.

In an art world that depends so heavily on photography, good slides of your best work can be instrumental in getting a show, winning a competition, or making a sale. In the fickle arena of the professional artist or craftsperson, photographs can even make the difference in a career. And in this era of such varied styles and schools, when a painting may be nothing more than a soft wash of color, accurate photographs are all the more important.

If you've ever tried to photo-graph your own artwork, chances are you've been disappointed with the result. Yet without the kind of information about materials and techniques this manual will provide, disappointment is inevitable. If you don't know how to match the proper film to your light source, your neutral gray field painting could end up as brown as an Old Master; if you don't compensate for the tendency of most cameras' exposure meters to render light subjects too dark, your pastel might lose its delicate highlights. Without a tripod, an etching's fine detail could succumb to camera "shake." The pitfalls are countless, but with this book at hand you can avoid them.

## YOU CAN DO IT

After repeated and unhappy attempts at producing good photos of their artwork (and often courting further disaster by coaxing a more "knowledgeable" friend to help), many artists resort to hiring a professional photographer. The cost of this can turn an unsuspecting sculptor or painter into the proverbial poor, starving artist. And in spite of the expense, the results can be unsatisfactory for the simple reason that the photographer doesn't understand the character of your work as well as you do. The fact is that you don't need the professional's extensive knowledge to make your photographs true to your art. This manual will streamline the task of photographing your artwork, assuming little prior knowledge on your part.

## WHAT YOU'LL NEED

The book will assume that you have access to a 35mm camera and that you're reasonably familiar with its operation. Preferably, it should be a camera that allows you some degree of manual control over exposure, or at least offers an exposure override mechanism. The compact, fully automatic 35mm snapshot cameras that are so popular now are not very well suited to photographing artwork, because they offer little or no exposure control, and their relatively wide-angle lenses are more likely to distort the artwork. Some of them can be used in a pinch, but single-lens reflex (SLR) cameras with their customary 50mm lenses are much more appropriate.

You'll also need a tripod. Both tripods and cameras can be rented or borrowed, if necessary, and one is no more or less necessary in photographing artwork well than the other. The case for the importance of the tripod is made in chapter 1; I recommend purchasing an inexpensive model. It will cost you less than half the minimum fee that most professional photographers charge, and prorated over many years, its cost is modest indeed.

Most of the information in the book applies to both two-dimensional and three-dimensional media, so read it all. The exceptions to this are chapters 3 and 4, which deal respectively with two- and three-dimensional work. You can skip the chapter that doesn't apply to you; any information that pertains to both kinds of work is repeated.

The book is primarily oriented toward making slides of artwork, as opposed to black and white or color prints, because nine times out of ten you'll be asked for slides. On that tenth occasion, a good color print can always be made from a slide. If you want to shoot color negative film and have a print produced from it, or if you need a black and white print for publicity purposes, refer to chapter 7, page 102, "Shooting Negative Film." This section will tell you what kinds of film to use, and how to go about having the prints made.

## ONE

**CAMERA AND TRIPOD**

## SLR VS. COMPACT AUTOMATIC (NON-SLR)

The 35mm single-lens-reflex (SLR) camera, top, lets you view your subject through the lens that will actually take the picture. It does this by means of a complex light-management system involving a mirror, a ground-glass screen, a five-sided prism, and secondary lenses. When you take the picture, the hinged mirror that reflects the subject image to the eyepiece flips up out of the way, allowing light to pass through the open shutter to the film.

The compact, fully automatic 35mm cameras (bottom) that are so popular these days work in a very different way. The subject is viewed through a window above and usually to the side of the lens, which sometimes causes a considerable disparity between what is seen and what is actually recorded on film. This may become a problem at the closer working distances often required in photographing artwork, although it can be anticipated and corrected for when composing.

The 35mm camera is available in an overwhelming variety of models, makes, and styles. Some let you view your subject through the camera's lens by reflecting its image off a hinged mirror to the eyepiece. In these cameras, called *single-lens reflexes* (SLRs), the mirror flips up out of the light's path when you push the shutter button to expose the film. Other cameras, such as the recently popular compact 35mm snapshot models, require that you view the subject through a separate window. These tend to be fully automatic in their functions, and, as mentioned in the Introduction, aren't as good for photographing artwork.

SLRs, on the other hand, range from manually controlled units to fully automatic ones, some of which will even focus for you. A few of the older models may not have a built-in light meter, which means that you will need to use a separate, hand-held meter. In describing the proper procedure for lighting an artwork and obtaining correct film exposure, I'll assume that you are using a camera with a built-in meter.

## MANUAL VS. AUTOMATIC EXPOSURE

The ideal camera for photographing artwork is one which allows you to set independently both the size of the lens aperture—often called the "f-stop"—and the duration of the exposure, commonly called the "shutter speed." Some cameras will set one or the other automatically to obtain proper exposure. An *aperture-priority* automatic camera sets the shutter speed after you choose the f-stop you want; a *shutter-priority* automatic sets the f-stop according to

what shutter speed you've selected. Most of the compact 35mm snapshot cameras, and many single-lens reflex models, now offer "programmed" systems in which both aperture and shutter speed are set automatically.

In photographing artwork, several problems can arise with these kinds of systems. The most serious is that the camera must make certain assumptions about the tones in your artwork, assumptions which may be invalid. These assumptions can cause your camera to misrepresent your artwork, rendering it too dark or too light.

If your artwork conforms to an automatic camera's expectations, then you may get a perfectly exposed slide. But most of the time your artwork won't be so obliging, so as a matter of practice you shouldn't rely on your camera's automatic exposure system. Many SLRs offer automatic and manual exposure modes; always use the manual option. If you're using a fully automatic shutter-priority or aperture-priority camera, the ways of overriding its exposure system will be explained in the sections on film exposure. NEVER use an automatic SLR in a program mode; use its aperture- or shutter-priority option, if one is offered.

### VIEWFINDER DISPLAYS
Cameras that permit manual exposure control will recommend the proper exposure for your film in numerous ways. Most of these involve displays that are visible in the camera's viewfinder, although some models also have displays on the outside of the camera as well. A system common in older cameras is the *match-needle,* in which you adjust either the aperture or the shutter speed until a moving

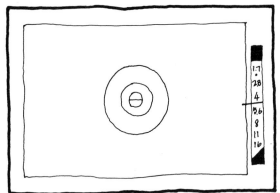

## THE SLR VIEWFINDER

Most camera's viewfinders display information about the aperture and shutter speeds being used, whether these are set manually or automatically. The design of such displays varies greatly, so refer to your camera manual for an explanation of how to interpret yours. In some cameras—particularly older models—"correct" exposure is obtained when you line a needle up on a site, by adjusting the shutter speed and/or aperture controls. This style of exposure control is called *match needle*, and one version of it is shown at top. Other cameras—usually newer models—substitute an *LED* (light-emitting diode) or *LCD* (liquid crystal display), in which you adjust controls to make a dot light up, or plus-and-minus symbols appear simultaneously. (An LED display is shown in the center.) In any of these systems, the shutter speed and/or aperture chosen are displayed at the edge of the frame. Automatic exposure systems also display this information in the viewfinder (bottom), but the camera chooses either the shutter speed, the aperture, or both automatically.

needle is centered in a site. In a similar design, one needle moves in response to the subject's light level, and you align a second needle with it. Newer cameras make use of *LED*s (light-emitting diodes) or *LCD*s (liquid crystal displays) to help you set the camera properly. An LED-style display, usually found on the right side of the viewfinder image, uses small color signals which change as you adjust the aperture or shutter speed. Proper exposure is obtained when the central signal, usually green, lights up. LCD displays are usually digital, and/or include plus and minus symbols (indicating over- and under-exposure).

In an automatic camera, or any camera set for automatic exposure, similar kinds of viewfinder displays provide information about which aperture and shutter speed have been set, even though you have no direct control over exposure. A shutter-priority camera will display the shutter speed you've chosen, along with the aperture it will set to obtain what it determines is correct exposure. An aperture-priority camera displays your chosen f-stop, as well as its automatically set shutter speed. If these cameras offer no manual exposure-control option, however, they won't have match-needle or diode-style indicators in the viewfinder.

Keep in mind that any camera's notion of "correct" exposure is subject to error. With an artwork filling its viewfinder, a camera set manually by any of the systems described above may produce the same kinds of exposure error as a camera operating with an automatic exposure system. The difference is that while the automatic camera is locked into its chosen exposure, a camera which lets you set both aperture and shutter speed manually will also let you ignore its recommendations, should they be unreliable, and take your picture even if the needle is unmatched or the wrong diode is glowing. This ability to second-guess the camera's light meter is very important in photographing artwork.

## THE LENS

A camera's lens projects the image of your artwork (or any other subject) onto the film surface, where it causes a chemical reaction in the light-sensitive emulsion of the film. Some cameras are designed so that the lens can be removed and interchanged with other lenses having compatible mounting hardware; in others, the lens is permanently attached to the camera body.

## THE NORMAL LENS

The 50mm lens supplied with 35mm SLRs is well suited to photographing works of art. "50mm" refers to the distance between the back of the lens and the film surface—called the lens' focal length—and should not be confused with the "35mm" camera, which refers to the metric width of the film the camera is made to shoot. A 50mm lens is sometimes called a *normal* lens because when you look through a 35mm SLR's viewfinder, it produces an image that appears to be the same size as the subject when the subject is seen with the unassisted eye.

## THE FIXED LENS

The fixed lens on most compact 35mm snapshot cameras is less effective in photographing artwork. It tends to be of shorter focal length—35 to 40mm—which means that it covers a wider angle of view, from the same camera position, than does the 50mm lens. As a result you have to get closer to your artwork to make it fill the

## LESS IS MORE: BUYING A CAMERA

The best camera for photographing works of art is usually the simplest. Simple not in the sense of requiring the least thought to operate—such cameras are actually more complex—but rather in the sense of having the fewest automatic features. More often than not, these features will trip you up when you try to use the camera to photograph your work, and they should be avoided when shopping for a camera that you intend to use for this purpose. Automation is one of the reasons the currently popular compact 35mm snapshot cameras are not well suited to photographing artwork. Choose a single-lens reflex (SLR) instead.

Although they will drive up the cost of an SLR substantially, automatic features are OK as long as the camera still has manual options. Make sure, for example, that autofocus cameras permit easy manual focusing, so that you can maximize the depth of the zone of sharpness in your photograph when shooting three-dimensional work. Even more important, choose a model that allows you to control both the lens aperture and shutter speed independently, and make sure that these controls are coupled to a viewfinder display that clearly indicates which settings will produce correct film exposure. Avoid cameras in which the only available exposure system sets one control automatically when you set the other, or sets both according to an exposure "program."

In most other respects, almost any 35mm SLR will work well in photographing artwork. Virtually all of them offer a system of interchangeable lenses, which opens up the possibility of substituting other lenses for the factory-issue 50mm, and of purchasing wide-angle, telephoto, or zoom lenses for special purposes, such as shooting installation views or controlling the way a three-dimensional piece is reproduced on film. The optical quality of most name-brand lenses is consistently good, and the mechanical and electronic components of most cameras stand up to all but the most heavy use. Some cameras, however, offer a limited range of slow shutter speeds, which may force you to use wider apertures than are advisable in photographing three-dimensional work. Be sure shutter speeds go down to at least one second.

## THE LENS

In addition to brand name and serial number, the engraved numbers and letters on the front or side of the lens tell you its focal length and maximum aperture. (Many lenses also indicate diameter of the front thread, usually with a ∅ symbol, so that you know what size filter accessories to buy.) The maximum aperture is expressed by a ratio—on the lens shown here, 1:2, for a maximum aperture of f2. Many current 50mm lenses have larger maximum apertures, such as f1.7 or f1.4. These apertures would be indicated by the ratios 1:1.7 and 1:1.4, respectively.

viewfinder, which may cause it to appear somewhat distorted in the final slide or print.

The closer working distances this kind of camera requires present another risk. Since you must view the artwork through a separate window offset from the lens, you won't see quite the same picture as the lens does. When you're within five or six feet of your artwork, this can cause it to be off-center in the finished slide or print. Smaller work that fits the viewfinder snugly may even end up cropped. Although some of these non-SLR cameras have marks in the viewfinder to help you adjust for this effect, in others you may have to adjust for it by eye after you've gotten your first results back. To do this, simply compare the slide to the way you originally composed the picture. If the artwork is shifted to one side, always frame it up shifted to the other side a like amount. But keep in mind that the closer you get to the artwork, the more extreme the difference will be.

It should be mentioned that many recent entries in the automatic compact camera market offer a "telephoto" setting for the lens, which is usually in the neigh-

borhood of a 70mm focal length. If you must use one of these cameras to photograph your work, choose the "tele" setting. This option, while it may minimize viewfinder discrepancies and subject distortion, does nothing to solve the exposure problems such cameras present.

## INTERCHANGEABLE LENSES

If you have an SLR with an interchangeable lens system, other lenses may be helpful in photographing certain kinds of artwork. *Wide-angle* lenses, while often useful for shooting installation views of exhibitions, make squaring up flat artwork much more difficult. A 50mm normal lens is much better for this purpose. But even the 50mm lens may on occasion misrepresent three-dimensional work, particularly if it's small. It may make the parts of the work closest to the camera— the curved side of a ceramic bowl, or the corner of a welded-metal construction—seem disproportionately large.

**Telephoto Lenses.** While changes in angle or composition can sometimes minimize this effect, a better way is to replace the 50mm lens with a lens of longer focal length, commonly called a *tele-*

ARTWORK     ARTWORK     ARTWORK

28 mm. Lens
"(WIDE-ANGLE)"

50 mm. Lens
"(NORMAL)"

105 mm. Lens
"(TELEPHOTO)"

## LENS FOCAL LENGTH

The focal length of a lens, which determines its angle of view, affects how close you must be to the artwork to make it fill the frame. This distance in turn affects the perspective with which the work is rendered. (See photographs on page 64 to see the effect of lens focal length on the proportions of a three-dimensional work.)

For most artwork, the 50mm lens your camera comes with is fine. For some sculptural work, though, a lens of longer focal length may keep the parts of the work in a more natural proportion to one another. A wide-angle lens, by contrast, is completely unsuited to photographing individual works of art. But the amount of space you have to work in may dictate your choice of lens—if you have the choice—rather than these aesthetic considerations.

*photo,* or "long" lens. In effect, this lens compresses the artwork, keeping its components more in proportion to each other as we see them with our much more sophisticated visual system. However, the lens' narrower angle of view requires that the camera be at a greater distance from the artwork, and this may not be possible in smaller spaces, particularly if the work is large. The "longer" the lens, the more room you'll need to work with. Lenses of 85mm to 105mm focal length should be adequate to prevent distortion in three dimensional artwork. If you have enough space, these lenses can also be used to photograph flat artwork, and they may even make squaring up the artwork easier.

**Zoom Lenses.** The ever-popular *zoom* lens may also be used to photograph artwork. It offers a continuous spectrum of focal lengths, within a certain range. By rotating a ring or sliding a collar on the lens, the user can pick and choose a focal length, tailoring it to the subject. Although zoom lenses are available in many different ranges, the most useful for photographing artwork range from wide-angle to moderate telephoto, such as 35-105mm or 28-85mm. In terms of focal length, zooms in this range are almost all-purpose lenses for photographing artwork because you can use their wide-angle settings for installation views and their normal and telephoto settings for individual works. However, these lenses often produce a dimmer viewfinder image than do lenses of fixed focal length, making framing and focusing in low light more difficult. If not well made, they may not produce as sharp an image as a fixed focal-length lens. Whether using a zoom lens or a lens of conventional design, avoid focal lengths of 135mm and above. This range can cause a

17

loss of a sense of volume in photographing three-dimensional artworks, and may require impractically large workspaces.

**Macro Lenses.** If your artwork is small, you may find that many of the lenses discussed above won't focus close enough to the work to make it fill the viewfinder frame. The longer the lens, the more likely it is that this will be a problem. While there are ways to adapt these lenses for use at closer distances (these will be discussed in the section on photographing small works in chapter 7), these may either reduce the sharpness of the photograph or disengage the automatic coupling of the lens to the camera body. Most manufacturers make lenses that are specially designed to focus at close distances, usually down to four or five inches from the subject. These are called *macro* lenses, and are available in a variety of focal lengths. The most common and useful ones are 50mm and 55mm, which provide the same angle of view as the normal lens that you probably have on your camera. In fact, a macro lens will focus from its closest distance to as far as the eye can see, like any lens of conventional design, and for this reason it can be used for general picture taking as well.

If you're in the market for a camera to photograph a lot of artwork, you may want to consider substituting a 50 or 55mm macro lens for the lens usually supplied with the camera, particularly if your work is flat or very small. This will elevate the cost of the package by as much as $100 or more, because a macro lens is considerably more expensive than a standard lens. Macros are designed to focus on a flat field, which is why they're so appropriate for two-dimensional work. Regular lenses, by contrast, focus on all points equidistant from the

## HOW TO CLEAN YOUR LENS

A frequent but frequently ignored reason for lack of sharpness in photographs is a dirty lens or filter. It's important to keep both clean to ensure that your artwork's finest details are recorded on the film.

To keep a lens dust-free, you may want to buy a photographic blower brush, or use a clean, soft camel's hair brush. For removing smudges and grease, you'll need to use photographic lens-cleaning tissue (the silicon-treated tissue for cleaning eyeglasses may leave a deposit on your lens surface) and a detergent cleaning solution intended for photographic lenses, such as that sold in small squeeze bottles by Kodak. Both are inexpensive and available in any photography store.

If your lens is removable, take it off and check the surface of the back element to see if it's clean, by holding it an an angle to a strong light source. Because it's protected, chances are it's OK, but give it a dusting at the least.

To clean either the back or front surface of the lens, blow on it lightly to remove any grit or dust that might scratch it, fold a sheet or two of lens cleaning tissue over on itself, moisten it with several drops of lens cleaning fluid, then apply it gently to the lens surface in a spiral motion, starting at the center of the lens and working your way out to the edges. Then take a dry tissue and polish the lens surface even more gently in the same way. Inspect the surface by holding it at an angle to the light, and repeat the cleaning if need be. Don't rub too hard, or you may abrade the thin anti-reflection coatings of optical plastic on the lens. If you have trouble removing streaks left after cleaning, try polishing them out with a cotton swab.

A glass filter can be cleaned the same way. Be sure to check the inside surface of the filter as well. NEVER try to clean an optical gelatin filter, should you use one. It can be scratched by the slightest pressure, and moisture can actually dissolve it or distort its flatness. Keep a gelatin filter in its protective packaging whenever you're not using it. (Filters will be covered in chapter 7, page 98.)

lens—in other words, a curved, hemispheric field.

**Macro-Zooms.** Many newer zoom lenses have similar close-focusing capabilities. Some of them shift into "macro" mode with a switch or a ring around the lens barrel that must be unlocked by pressing a button; in other "macro" zooms, the focusing ring's close-focusing range is increased at certain focal lengths. It's important to choose small lens apertures when using a zoom lens this way, particularly if you are setting it to the longer focal lengths of its range.

## THE LENS APERTURE

All lenses contain a diaphragm of metal blades that form an aperture which can be made smaller or larger by turning a ring on the lens barrel. The numbers on the ring represent openings of different size and are called "f-stops." In addition to their effect on film exposure, these openings also determine how much of your artwork (in addition to the specific point at which you've focused) will be in focus when you take the picture. This zone of sharpness is known as the "depth of field," and its size can have a strong effect on the way your artwork is rendered, particularly if it is three dimensional. The proper lens aperture can vary considerably with the nature of your work, so it will be discussed further as it pertains to specific kinds of artwork.

## THE TRIPOD

The most fabulous camera in the world can't guarantee good photographs of your artwork. A *tripod* is the tool that assures a successful photograph. In fact, most of the problems that artists experience in photographing their work stem from having hand-held the camera. You *must* use a tripod because:

1. Even if you have nerves of steel, the strength of your light source ordinarily won't be sufficient to permit shutter speeds fast enough to prevent camera movement, or "shake" as it's known in the lingo. And although camera shake may not cause a visibly blurred image, it can reduce the sharpness of your slide or print considerably. A tripod allows you to use slower shutter speeds without ill effect.
2. The fixed camera position that the tripod affords is the only way you can be sure your artwork is perfectly centered in the viewfinder at the moment of exposure, and in the case of traditional two-dimensional work, that it appears "square"—i.e., that its corners form right angles and that its sides are of equal length. The tripod is the only means by which you can apply a system to the task of "squaring up" two-dimensional work.
3. Many techniques in photographing both two- and three-dimensional work require a rigid camera position to build light-baffling or reflecting materials around.
4. Existing-light views of an exhibition or of work *in situ* indoors can only be made with a tripod, because of the slower shutter speeds low light levels require.

You can dispense with the tripod on some occasions, such as in photographing work outdoors. Don't try to get around using a tripod, however, by dragging your artwork outside to photograph it. Natural light is difficult if not impossible to control, and may pose color problems such as those described in chapter 2. Even in bright light, though, it's a good idea to use a tri-

**THE TRIPOD**
The tripod before extension of legs.

The tripod head.

The tripod with center post extended.

The tripod head with platform fully tilted.

The cable release.

pod; it's an effective compositional aid, and a way to keep a set of slides consistent.

## WHAT TO LOOK FOR

Good lightweight tripods are available for as little as forty to fifty dollars. They can also be rented for as little as five dollars a day, or borrowed from more well-equipped friends. But before you buy a tripod, you should put it through its paces.

First of all, the model you select should be stable when its telescoping legs are fully extended. To test it, press down on the top to see how much it gives or wobbles. Its feet will grip some surfaces more securely than others.

**Control Levers.** The tripod should also have complete, accessible, and easily manipulated controls at its *head,* where you mount the camera. These include two levers at right angles, one to tilt the camera forward and backward, the other to tilt it from side to side. Most such levers will lock into position when twisted; some may require tightening a separate nut, a more awkward design. The tripod head should also rotate independently of the sliding post it is mounted on, and you should be able to lock in its position with an adjacent nut. Make sure the tripod *has* a sliding post, because it is the only means by which you can raise or lower the camera without adjusting the legs, and is an important control in squaring up two-dimensional artwork. It locks into position with a knurled ring just below where the tripod's legs connect to its head, or with a nut on the side of the head.

**Vertical Tilt.** Finally, be certain you can tilt the tripod's camera platform to a fully vertical position. This is usually done with the lever that controls the head's side-to-side motion. Some tripods won't

tilt all the way; you'll end up compensating for this fault by overextending the tripod's opposing leg, and all height adjustments will shift the image laterally because the sliding post will no longer be vertical. This capability is less of an issue if your work is flat, because it's easier to shoot a vertical piece on its side with the camera horizontal. But if you have to shoot a two-dimensional vertical piece as it hangs on a gallery wall, or if you're photographing free-standing vertical objects, obviously the camera must be vertical too.

You need to keep a few other things in mind when shopping for a tripod. One is to be sure it has enough extension so you can raise the camera to a height that is level with the midpoint of your artwork, whether it's a standing sculpture or a painting. For example, even if you photograph them resting on the floor against a wall, very large paintings may require that the camera be elevated considerably above eye level, which some tripods won't permit. You can obtain some of this extension with the sliding post, but if you overextend the column you may sacrifice some camera steadiness, and limit the kinds of adjustments you can make when you square the work up.

Larger, pricier tripods may have geared center posts which you can raise and lower with a crank. This design is overkill for a 35mm camera, and invites damage to your tripod should you drop it. The fewer knobs and other protrusions the tripod has, the more likely it will last. Tripods also have a variety of leg-extension and locking gimmicks, but the most practical choice is probably a conventional telescoping tubular design with knurled knobs.

## THE CABLE RELEASE

At the slow shutter speeds a tripod permits, a *cable release* is an indispensible accessory. It allows you to trip the shutter without the risk of camera movement that pressing the shutter button with your finger creates. The cable release is a flexible cord with a sliding cable running through it. Its tapered end is screwed into the threaded opening in the camera's shutter button; the plunger on the other end is held between the index and middle finger. Depressing the plunger with the thumb fires the shutter.

Practice with the cable release before you load and shoot your film. Always push the cable release's plunger down gradually, holding the plunger end so that the cable itself is gently flexed. If you keep the cable too taut, you may yank the camera during the exposure. Longer cable releases minimize this risk, but tend to get their internal spring fouled up more easily. A good compromise is a cable release around a foot long.

If you'd prefer not to buy a cable release, you can use your camera's self-timer (if it has one) to trip the shutter. Set it for as long an interval as possible, to let any vibrations created by setting it subside. However, this method of firing the shutter makes the business of taking repeated shots of an artwork far more time-consuming. A cable release costs anywhere from a few dollars to as much as ten, depending on its length and quality, and it's worth every penny.

A tripod and cable release are indispensible in photographing works of art. But we might add one item to the list of reasons to buy them: it gives you a tax-deductible excuse to buy something you may have fancied for your own dalliance in photography.

---

### SUMMARY/ **CAMERA AND TRIPOD**

- An SLR (single-lens reflex) is the best 35mm camera for photographing artwork because it lets you view the subject through the lens, rather than a separate window.
- Because the light-metering system in your camera is prone to error, it's best to use an SLR that offers manual exposure control when photographing artwork.
- Automatic exposure systems can be used in photographing artwork only if they offer provisions for overriding the programmed exposure.
- Both manual and automatic exposure systems make use of viewfinder displays, either to help you determine the proper exposure, or to tell you what settings the camera has chosen.
- Most SLRs are supplied with a 50mm "normal" lens, but offer a system of interchangeable lenses.
- The fixed, relatively wide-angle lens on many compact 35mm snapshot cameras can distort an artwork.
- Telephoto lenses may be used to minimize distortion in three-dimensional work.
- Zoom lenses can take the place of a number of fixed focal-length lenses, because they offer a continuous range of focal lengths.
- Macro lenses are useful in photographing artwork because they focus much closer than conventional lenses, and focus on the flat plane formed by two-dimensional work, rather than a curve.
- A dirty lens can cause a dramatic reduction in the sharpness of your photograph.
- The variable diaphragm inside your lens controls both exposure and the depth of the zone of sharpness in your photographs.
- The tripod is as essential in photographing artwork well as the camera itself.
- The tripod's head should be attached to a sliding post, and must have complete tilting and rotating capability. It should have adequate height when fully extended.
- The tripod should always be used with a cable release.

The time-honored notion that natural light is best to paint by and truest to color has led many artists to photograph their work by daylight, usually near a window or in open shade outdoors. But while daylight may seem the most pleasing light source to artist and layman alike, photographic film doesn't see things the way we do. The brain constantly tunes the human visual system to different sources of light; color films, on the other hand, are made to record accurate color only in a certain kind of light, and are said to be *balanced* for that light.

### THE COLOR OF LIGHT
The film that most people use, whether for snapshots or for photographing their artwork, is in fact balanced for daylight. But for photographic purposes, daylight is rather strictly defined as light having the characteristics of direct sunlight. This includes the light from electronic flash units, which professional photographers often use to photograph works of art. Such professional units are specifically designed for studio use, and are much more powerful than the kind of compact device you would mount on your camera for snapshots. *Never* use a camera-mounted flash unit to photograph a work of art; even if the work doesn't dissolve in a sea of glare, it will have a flat, dull appearance. Never use undiffused sunlight as a light source, either, because of its strong directionality and unevenness.

To avoid these problems, many artists choose to photograph their work by indirect sunlight, which is certainly a much more even form of natural light. But because the light from a window or in the open shade

has clear sky as its primary source, *daylight* film—designed for the warm, direct rays of the sun itself—will often render it with a strong blue cast in the finished slide, a frequent complaint of do-it-yourself artwork photographers. If you must shoot slides by daylight, do so on an overcast day, and use corrective filtration on the camera, as described in the section on filters in chapter 7. For photographing works of art, though, far better results can be obtained with controlled *tungsten* light, and film balanced for this light.

### COLOR TEMPERATURE
In photography, light is described by its *color temperature* on the Kelvin scale, or degrees Celsius above absolute zero. This has nothing to do with the actual heat of a particular light source, but rather with the color emitted by a hot object, which gets bluer as the object gets hotter. At 5500 degrees, the color it emits corresponds to that of sunlight; this is the color temperature of the light that daylight film is "balanced" for. It's understandable, then, why daylight film records the light in open shade or from a window on a sunny day as bluish: blue skylight has a color temperature of nearly 12000 degrees Kelvin. At the other extreme, daylight film renders subjects illuminated by artificial incandescent light with a strong brownish-yellow cast, because the color temperature of the light that a tungsten filament emits—about 3200 degrees on the Kelvin scale—is considerably lower than the 5500 degree light that daylight film is designed for. If you've ever taken pictures on daylight film by studio floodlights, this cast is probably all too familiar to you.

### TUNGSTEN-BALANCED FILMS
Many people aren't aware that some slide films are made specifically for use in tungsten light—the kind of light we illuminate our homes with. In tungsten light, tungsten-balanced color film will render blues blue and reds red, and will reproduce whites and grays without an unnatural color cast. For this reason, we'll be using tungsten-balanced films to make slides of your artwork.

Like natural light, tungsten light varies somewhat in its color temperature, although to a much lesser degree. Lower wattage bulbs such as those we use in lamps have an even lower color temperature than the 3200 degrees that tungsten films are balanced for—as low as 2600 degrees Kelvin. Even tungsten-balanced films may give this kind of light a slightly yellowish rendition, which is rarely objectionable for general-purpose photography but may misrepresent the colors of an artwork. The brighter the lightbulb, generally the closer its color temperature will be to 3200 degrees. But even if you use 500-watt floodlamps to illuminate your studio, the light will still be a bit lower in color temperature than tungsten film is balanced for. For this reason, we'll be buying special bulbs that are manufactured to produce light of a very specific color temperature.

**Type A and Type B.** Tungsten film balanced for 3200 degree light is sometimes called *Type B* film. This designation is really only used to distinguish it from one other film, a tungsten-balanced version of Kodak's Kodachrome slide film identified by the code letters *KPA*. Kodachrome KPA is balanced for light with a color temperature of

3400 degrees Kelvin, a slightly bluer light than any other tungsten film is designed for. It is sometimes called *Type A* film, but we will call it tungsten Kodachrome or KPA. Kodachrome KPA is a sharp fine-grained film, well suited to photographing individual works of art. It is not an appropriate choice for interior installation views, because the tungsten lighting typical of exhibition areas is considerably lower in color temperature than the 3400 degree light the film is balanced for.

Several other 35mm tungsten-balanced slide films are suitable for photographing artwork. These are Kodak's tungsten Ektachromes. They are balanced for 3200 degree light, rather than the 3400 degree light for which tungsten Kodachrome is designed. And as this book was going to press, Fuji Photographic introduced its own 35mm tungsten-balanced slide film, the first suitable alternative to Kodak's tungsten slide films for photographing artwork. Called Fujichrome 64T (code RPT), the film gave excellent results in initial tests. Although it is unlikely to be as widely available as the Kodak films, artists who can get it may want to try it and compare it to the results they get with Ektachrome. The film is actually balanced for a slightly lower color temperature than the Ektachrome films—3100 degrees Kelvin rather than 3200 degrees. Because this color balance is closer to that of ordinary tungsten light, the film is better for shooting individual artworks by the existing floodlighting of galleries and studios.

The difference between the Kodak and Fuji films goes beyond their color balances, however; the slides they produce have a noticeably different appearance, at least when looked at side by side. The color of both tungsten- and daylight-balanced Fujichrome is more *saturated* (a photographer's term for brighter and richer) than that of the Ektachromes—some would say unnaturally so. Fujichrome 64T also produces more contrast between lighter and darker areas than the Ektachromes, resulting in a "snappier" slide. The Ektachromes produce a subtler overall effect; Kodachrome KPA probably falls somewhere in between.

In theory, each kind of film described above will produce "neutral" color in the kind of light it is balanced for. In this respect, each can be depended on to yield a slide that is a reasonable facsimile of your artwork. In practice, though, the characteristics of one film may be better suited to the qualities of your artwork than another. And although this book was written with Kodak films in mind, it should be said that Fuji's new entry is a workable and welcome alternative and can fill in for the Kodak films that this book often assumes you are using.

## FILM SPEED

A film's ISO rating—often called its *speed*—is an index or measurement of its sensitivity to the kind of light it is balanced for. When a camera's ISO control is set to the correct number for the film in use, its meter knows how much light that particular film must receive to produce a properly exposed slide or negative. The higher a film's ISO number, the more sensitive it is to light; it needs less light than a film with a lower ISO number to produce a correctly exposed picture.

While some newer 35mm cameras set the film's ISO automatically according to an optical code on the film cartridge, most still require that you set it manually, usually with a dial on or near the camera's rewind crank. Although some of the techniques involved in using fully automatic cameras to photograph artwork may require the use of a different ISO setting than the manufacturer recommends, as we'll see, you should be sure that the film's ISO is set correctly initially, so that the light meter in your camera knows how much exposure to recommend.

**Slow Films.** The films we will be using have lower ISOs than the films you're probably accustomed to shooting in general-purpose photography. Tungsten Kodachrome has an ISO of 40. Tungsten Ektachrome comes in ISO 50 (code letters EPY) and ISO 160 (code letters EPT and ET). Fujichrome 64T, as its name suggests, has an ISO rating of 64, making it slightly more sensitive to light than Ektachrome 50. Films with low ISO numbers, whether color or black and white, slide or negative, are best for photographing individual works of art in controlled light because they produce sharper, more fine-grained images than the higher-speed films. In these circumstances, tungsten Ektachrome 50, Fujichrome 64T, or tungsten Kodachrome (with its ISO of 40) is a better choice than High-Speed tungsten Ektachrome. High-Speed tungsten Ektachrome's ISO of 160 does make it useful for shooting installation views and individual works in existing gallery light, and occasionally for photographing three-dimensional work when you need good depth of field and your lighting is limited. Its appearance will be somewhat grainier than that of Ektachrome 50 if the slide is projected or enlarged. Ektachrome 160's extra sensitivity to light is usually unnecessary when you photograph your individual works of art, because you will be flooding them with artificial light, and using a tripod, which permits longer exposures.

One advantage to the Ektachrome and Fujichrome films—either tungsten- or daylight-balanced—is that they may be "push"-processed by the color lab or photo finisher. This special treatment allows you to set a higher ISO than the manufacturer recommends for a film, which may be useful when relatively low light limits your shooting options, as explained later. Refer to chapter 7, page 104, for more information about pushing film.

In theory, each kind of film described here will produce "neutral" results in the kind of light it is balanced for, and in this respect will be "true" to your artwork. In practice, however, your work may be better served by one film than another. It might be worth the investment in the two different kinds of lamps these films require (described later) to determine which film seems to produce the most agreeable result.

## AMATEUR AND PROFESSIONAL FILMS

Most manufacturers make films in both "amateur" and "professional" types. Amateur films are designed to sit on a camera store shelf at room temperature for prolonged periods; professional films, on the other hand, are "aged" by the manufacturer until tests indicate their color balance and other characteristics are optimum, at which time they are refrigerated until sold. Ektachrome 50 EPY, Ektachrome 160 EPT and Fujichrome 64T are professional films, and professional photo suppliers should have them stored in a refrigerator. (Ektachrome 160 is also available in an amateur version, code ET; Ektachrome 50 and Fujichrome 64T are

## THE 81A FILTER

Even in the best of circumstances, certain slide films have a tendency to "go blue." And it's generally acknowledged that given the choice, most people prefer warm colors to cool ones, whether in their living rooms or their slides. For this reason, it's a good idea to use a warming filter over the camera lens when shooting your artwork, particularly if it has light or pastel tones. If you keep the filter on the lens when you take your light reading, the meter should compensate for the very slight degree to which it cuts back the light reaching the film.

Filters that produce a slight warming effect are usually described by their Kodak proprietary designation—the Wratten #81 series. Of these, an 81A filter is perhaps the most useful. If it proves too strong, you can substitute an 81, or if too mild, an 81B. See the color plates on pages 112 and 113 for an illustration of these filters' effects.

Try to buy glass-mounted, screw-in type filters, so that you can clean them should they become smudged or dirty. They usually cost less than ten dollars, depending on their type and diameter. Make sure you buy them in a size that fits the front thread of your lens barrel, the diameter of which is usually indicated in millimeters on the front of the lens. (Don't confuse this number with the focal length of the lens.) You can also buy these filters in square "gelatins" from Kodak, but gelatin filters can't be cleaned, are quite delicate, and must be attached to the lens with an accessory mounting bracket, although you can improvise a cardboard frame for them and tape it to the lens. They are also just as expensive as glass filters. Read the section on filters in chapter 7 for more details.

only available as a professional film. Kodachrome KPA, although described as a professional film by Kodak, is usually not refrigerated.) Unless you plan to use a professional film immediately, you should keep it in your refrigerator, too. Allow at least an hour for the film to warm up before you use it, so that no condensation forms on the film surface in the camera. If you buy a large quantity of film (either for the sake of consistency or economy) you may want to freeze it, in which case you should allow several hours for thawing. And if you don't intend to take your exposed film to the lab or photo finisher the next morning, put it back in the refrigerator, *in its plastic canister,* after you shoot it. Professional films are more sensitive to the ill effects of heat and age than are amateur films, so be especially careful with them. Improper storage and handling may cause changes in color, contrast, and speed.

**Effective Speed.** While all manufacturers test the speed of their professional films before releasing them for sale, some of them—notably Kodak—will actually admit it when a specific batch of film varies from the emulsion's official ISO. Kodak calls the true ISO of a given batch of film its *effective speed,* and prints it in red on the poop sheet supplied with the film. Kodak's tungsten Ektachrome EPY, with a nominal ISO of 50, can have on occasion an effective speed of 64 or 40. Professional Ektachrome EPT, Kodak's high-speed tungsten slide film, sometimes tests at ISO 200 in spite of its official ISO of 160. These variations are not great enough to cause big differences in your slides (which is why some manufacturers of professional daylight-balanced films choose to ignore them), and more often than not a professional film's effective speed is the same as its advertised ISO. Kodachrome KPA, for example, has no effective speed advisory. But if you're using the Professional Ektachrome films, you should always check the poop sheet for the film's effective speed, and set your camera's ISO control accordingly.

## FILM PROCESSING

The tungsten Ektachrome films require the same kind of processing as their daylight cousins, a treatment described by the Kodak proprietary name of *E-6.* (Fujichrome 64T can also be processed in E-6 chemistry.) It's available at professional photography labs and commercial photo finishers. Photography shops will simply send your film to one of these operations, then mark up the price, so it's better to patronize the lab itself, if it does reliable work. Labs and commercial photo finishers can often turn these films around in several hours, so that if you live near one you can shoot a test roll and have it processed while your setup is still intact. If your film has to be sent off, it may be a couple of days before you get it back.

Tungsten Kodachrome film, or KPA, is processed in an entirely different way, a method which is a closely guarded secret. Whether you take the film to a lab or a photography store, it will have to be sent to a Kodak processing facility, and usually takes a couple of days to get back, depending on where you live. You can ask the store or lab proprietor to put the film in the rush bag. Kodak makes no guarantees for this service, but you can sometimes get your film back in a day if you live near a processing facility or in a large city. Kodak will also process its Ektachrome slide films, but the same turnaround times apply.

## BASIC LIGHTING HARDWARE

A clip-on light fixture. (If you feel extravagant, you can buy light stands which accept the metal sleeve on certain fixtures, or to which you can simply clip the fixtures.)

## LIGHTS

Although tungsten-balanced films will produce far more accurate color in any level of tungsten light than daylight film, it's best not to use the ordinary bulbs you may have on hand to light your work. As mentioned, these don't provide the precise color temperature of light that tungsten films are calibrated for, so you should purchase color-balanced bulbs such as those described below. (If you must use ordinary bulbs, Fujichrome 64T may produce a less yellowish result than tungsten Ektachrome.) You may already have *clip-on light fixtures,* however, and you'll need at least two of these, particularly if you're shooting flat work. Be sure that they're designed to accept a 500-watt lamp. *Don't* use fixtures with paper-lined sockets, or ones with questionable wiring.

## PHOTOFLOODS

There are two basic styles, or profiles, of *photoflood* lamp, the bulbs specifically made for color photographic work. One, which we'll call a *standard* photoflood lamp, is shaped like a conventional lightbulb. Because this kind of bulb gives off light in all directions, you need a metal *reflector* (two or more for flat work) to concentrate and aim the light. Whether you buy or use your own light fixtures, be sure they have an outside thread onto which you can screw the reflector. The light from a standard photoflood bulb with a metal reflector tends to be less even than that from a *reflector photoflood,* which is a conical bulb with a fairly long stem and a built-in reflector. The reflector-style photoflood lamp may make it somewhat easier to light the surface of a drawing, print, or painting evenly.

Unfortunately, reflector photofloods are considerably more expensive than standard-profile pho-

## BULB PROFILES
The reflector photoflood lamp, A, requires no separate reflector, but is considerably more expensive than a standard lightbulb-style photoflood, B. If you opt for the latter, you will need to buy metal reflectors, C, which screw into the thread on the clip-on fixture.

toflood bulbs, although you do save the price of separate reflectors. They will cost you anywhere from $9.50 to $12.50, while a standard photoflood lamp will cost only $2.50 to $3.50. Reflectors cost anywhere from four to seven dollars apiece, depending on their size. The bigger ones (ten to twelve inches in diameter) will provide broader light. The light produced by a standard photoflood lamp in a reflector is somewhat brighter than that produced by a reflector photoflood.

**Wattage and Color Temperature.** Both reflector photofloods and standard-profile color-rated lamps are available in various wattages. Unless your work is small and you can place your lights close to it, the 500-watt bulbs are the most practical choice. (You can always back them away from the work if they seem too hot.) The 500-watt reflector photoflood lamp that produces 3200 degree light (the light the tungsten Ektachromes are balanced for and that you should use with Fujichrome 64T) is known by the code letters EAL, which are the same whether or not the bulb is manufactured by Westinghouse, GE, or Sylvania. This bulb has a frosted front face, which further diffuses the light. The standard-profile 500-watt 3200 degree bulb goes by the code ECT.

These combinations of profile and wattage are also available in a bulb with a color temperature of 3400 degrees Kelvin, specifically for use with tungsten Kodachrome KPA. Be sure you don't mix them up, though; while using 3200 degree bulbs with KPA may produce a slight, unobjectionable warmth, using 3400 degree bulbs with the tungsten Ektachrome films will result in a bluish cast in your slides. The 500-watt reflector photoflood

for use with tungsten Kodachrome goes by the code letters DXC. The standard-profile 3400 degree bulbs go by EBV for the 500-watt version.

**Burn Time.** Any of these color rated lamps has a more limited useful life than the kinds of bulbs we light our living spaces with, but even this varies considerably from bulb to bulb. The EAL bulb has a "rated life" of fifteen hours; the DXC and EBV only six hours. The ECT bulb has a rated life of sixty hours. A bulb's rated life is the amount of burn time for which the bulb's color temperature is guaranteed; the bulb may actually last much longer. The bulb's useful life may be further limited by the buildup of carbon on the inside, gradually reducing its brightness, and by turning the lamp on and off excessively. Keep careful track of the amount of time you actually have the bulb on; write it down on the bulb's packaging, to avoid confusion. Don't leave the bulbs on needlessly, and don't use them for general illumination, particularly the reflector photofloods (they're too expensive). Also, don't mix old and new bulbs, particularly in a flat copy setup. In spite of the limited lifespans of these bulbs, if you're judicious in their use, they should last for many photo sessions.

Because these bulbs are extremely hot when they're on, they can set flammable materials on fire if within a couple of feet of them for a long enough period. Again, the bulbs should be used only in fixtures designed for high wattage. The type of fixture sold in photography stores is usually meant for this kind of use, and has a wooden handle so that you can aim the lamp when it's on without burning yourself.

**WHERE TO BUY EQUIPMENT**
The films described above, as well

as the photographic lamps made specifically for use with them, are generally only available in a well-supplied photographic store that caters to a professional clientele. If you're not in any hurry, you may be able to special-order them through a less well-stocked outfit. In a pinch, regular tungsten bulbs of as high wattage as possible, and the "amateur" version of Kodak's High Speed Ektachrome 160 (ET), will suffice, and can be obtained from hardware stores and suburban camera shops. Clip-on light fixtures and metal reflectors can be purchased either at camera stores or hardware and lighting outlets.

**Advanced Lighting Options.** If you find yourself photographing your work extensively, you may want to consider purchasing professional quartz lights. Quartz lights come in a variety of styles and are priced anywhere from fifty to two hundred dollars apiece, depending on features. A good part of the cost is the tungsten-halogen bulb itself, which burns as long as 150 hours, and never varies from its rated color temperature. These lights are available only through a professional photography dealer. Be sure to ask the dealer about their proper treatment and use. Among other things, you should never touch the bulb itself; any oil on its surface could cause it to fail or even shatter. The most commonly used bulbs produce 1000 watts, and burn even hotter than 500-watt floodlamps.

Another advanced lighting option is electronic flash. Preferred by many professional photographers, "strobe" light is the same color temperature as daylight, so daylight film is used with it rather than tungsten film. Because the illumination electronic flash provides is instantaneous, it doesn't subject delicate artworks to the kind of heat that tungsten light generates. And because relatively fast shutter speeds may be used with it, you don't have to worry as much about competing ambient light. While a few 35mm flash systems may permit the kinds of lighting arrangements described in this manual, you will still need an expensive, specialized meter to measure the evenness of the light. Professional-level strobe hardware is extremely expensive, something best left to the professional you've decided not to hire.

## COMPETING LIGHT SOURCES

Because you'll be using continuous tungsten light and relatively long exposures (slow shutter speeds) to photograph your work, you'll have to eliminate any other ambient light sources that might affect the evenness or color of your result. Windows open to the sky must be covered with opaque cloth or plastic; if you work in a window-filled loft, it may be easier to shoot at night. Former industrial spaces often have fluorescent lighting, and because it's not particularly bright, it's easy to forget to turn it off before shooting. Depending on your exposures, if left on it can contribute a noticeable greenish cast to your pictures. If you're using regular tungsten bulbs to throw extra light on the piece for framing and focusing, be sure to turn them off as well. (Don't worry—you'll be reminded of all this later, when you're actually ready to expose your film.)

## THE EXPOSURE EQUATION: SHUTTER SPEED, LENS APERTURE, AND YOUR CAMERA'S METER

As you've learned, different films have different sensitivities to light, indicated by their ISO numbers. You must always adjust your cam-

### THE SHUTTER SPEED

Usually this control is mounted on the top of the camera, but on some models it is a ring around the lens mount. Shutter speed—the length of time the curtain covering the film is open—is one of the two ways in which the amount of light reaching the film is controlled. (In some cameras, the shutter is a metal diaphragm inside the lens, separate from and not to be confused with the lens aperture diaphragm.)

era's film speed setting to the proper ISO. It's the only way the camera's metering system will know how much light the film needs for proper exposure—that is, to produce a slide that is neither too dark nor too light.

## SHUTTER SPEED

The amount of light that reaches the film is controlled by two mechanisms. One is the *shutter,* which is a cloth or metal curtain in front of the film (or sometimes a diaphragm of metal leaves in the lens) that uncovers the film for a precisely timed period—anywhere from $1/1000$ or $1/2000$ of a second to one, two, four, eight, or more seconds. The slower the shutter speed, the more light reaches the film through the lens opening. Each change in shutter speed represents a doubling or halving of this time, and consequently of the light that is allowed to pass to the film. In a manual camera, an automatic camera in a manual mode, or a shutter-priority automatic camera, you set shut-

aperture
ring

f-stops

## THE APERTURE RING

The aperture ring on the lens barrel adjusts the size of the aperture inside the lens to control the amount of light reaching the film. The numbers on the ring represent the size of the openings, called f-stops.

ter speed with a control usually on the top deck of the camera.

## LENS APERTURE

The other mechanism that controls the amount of light reaching the film is the *lens aperture*. The aperture is a variable opening formed by metal blades inside the lens itself. You change its size by adjusting a ring on the lens barrel, usually close to where the lens connects to the camera body. Each number on the ring—2, 2.8, 11, 16—represents a different-sized opening, often called an *f-stop*. The larger the f-stop, the more light can reach the film in a given amount of time, or shutter speed. The confusing thing is that the smaller the f-stop number, the larger the opening; f2, as it's designated, is twice as large as f2.8; f11 is twice as large an opening as f16. Study the lens barrel to see the sequence. (If you take the lens off the camera, you can see the aperture open and close as you turn the ring; alternatively, depress your camera's depth of field preview button, if it has one, as you turn the aperture ring.) Each of these changes in aperture will produce the same change in exposure that a similar adjustment in shutter speed will. For example, if you wanted to increase your exposure, you could use either a slower shutter speed—e.g., change from $1/8$ second to $1/4$ second—or a wider aperture, f5.6 instead of f8.

## WHAT THE LIGHT METER TELLS YOU

When measuring light, your camera's meter arrives at various combinations of aperture and shutter speed that it thinks will produce a good exposure on film with the ISO number you've set. In a programmed automatic camera or a camera in "program" mode, this combination is set automatically. In an aperture-priority or shutter-priority automatic camera, you set one and the camera sets the other. In a manual camera, you set both according to the signals the camera provides.

It's important to understand that you can obtain the same exposure with various combinations of shutter speed and aperture. You'll observe this as you change one or the other on your camera, whether it's an automatic or a manual. Imagine that you're photographing a meadow, and you've set a shutter speed of 1/125 second. With an ISO 100 film, the camera selects (in the case of a shutter-priority automatic) or advises (in a manual camera) an f-stop of f11. Suddenly you see a horse galloping across the meadow, and you decide to increase the shutter speed to 1/250 second to better freeze the movement of the horse. But this cuts in half the amount of time the light has to strike the film, so the camera will in turn select or advise an f-stop of f8, a larger opening which admits twice as much light as f11 in a given period, in order to give the film the same amount of exposure to light. You could even choose a shutter speed of 1/500 second, which would necessitate an even wider aperture of f5.6. Other combinations of f-stop and shutter speed that would produce this same exposure (though they'd be too slow to stop the horse's motion) are 1/60 second at f16 or 1/30 second at f22.

A film of a given ISO always needs more or less the same amount of light to produce a well-exposed negative or slide. Yet in general purpose photography, light levels differ dramatically from subject to subject, depending on whether you're indoors or out, or whether it's bright or overcast. This is why you need the kind of wide-ranging control that the lens aperture and shutter provide. A certain film may require an exposure of 1/250 second at f16 in bright outdoor light, but need a much slower shutter speed of 1/60 second and a very wide aperture of f2 to produce the same film exposure in dim indoor light.

## FILM SPEED AND THE LIGHT READING

A film of a different ISO, however, needs more or less light than another film to produce a properly exposed slide or print of a subject with a given light level, and this directly affects the combination of aperture and shutter speed that your camera's meter recommends or sets. Because a film with an ISO of 50 has only half the sensitivity to light of one with an ISO of 100, your camera's meter will set or recommend either a one-stop wider aperture or a one-stop slower shutter speed to double the amount of light reaching the film. In a situation requiring an exposure of 1/250 second at f8 with an ISO 100 film, an ISO 50 film would require an exposure either of 1/125 second at f8, or 1/250 second at f5.6. (Your camera will tell you this if you change the ISO setting while pointing at the same subject.) If, on the other hand, you were to use a film with an ISO of 200—with twice the sensitivity of the ISO 100 film—the camera would indicate proper exposures (i.e., combinations of f-stop and shutter speed) of either 1/500 second at f8 or 1/250 second at f11.

You're less likely to encounter the variety of shooting situations and light levels that the 35mm camera is designed for in photographing artwork. With the exception of work that must be photographed *in situ*, our conditions will be more consistent: we will be setting up our own lights, using the relatively slow shutter speeds that a tripod permits, and avoiding very wide lens apertures.

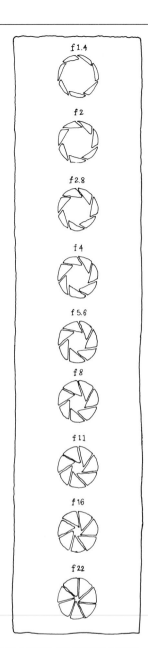

## THE LENS DIAPHRAGM

The numbers on the aperture control ring of your lens represent different-size openings formed by the diaphragm of metal leaves inside the lens. The size of this opening is one of the two ways in which the amount of light reaching the film is controlled, the shutter speed being the other. A larger opening—indicated by a smaller number—lets in more light; a smaller opening, indicated by a larger number, lets in less light. The smallest number represents the largest aperture you can get with your particular lens.

The most common mistake of artists who photograph their own work is in allowing their camera's light metering system, whether manual or automatic, to have the final word on what exposure the film will receive. The problem with this is that the light meter in your camera assumes that the tones, or brightnesses in your subject—whether it's your artwork or your Uncle Fred—will average out to a medium gray value. This is often true of a general scene with a variety of surfaces, and evenly distributed highlights and shadows, which is why the system works fairly reliably in general purpose photography. But these assumptions are far less often true of an artwork.

The camera's exposure system will set or recommend a combination of f-stop and shutter speed that will render any given value as a medium gray in your slide or print. If you fill its viewfinder with a white wall, for example, it will choose an exposure that will represent that wall as a medium gray instead. Even if a person is standing in front of the wall, enough of it may be registered to throw off the exposure substantially, causing the figure to be underexposed. The camera will make the same mistake in determining exposure for artworks that are primarily light in tone, such as a watercolor of pastel hues, or a pale marble sculpture. It will underexpose these subjects if you let it.

Conversely, if you allow the camera to set the exposure (or, if you're using a manual camera, you use the exposure it recommends) for a very dark subject—perhaps a minimalist painting of deep, subtly different values and colors of near-black—it will make those dark tones gray in the final photograph, by overexposing them.

## THE GRAY CARD

If the tones in your artwork happen to average out to the medium gray the camera's meter is calibrated for, then you might well obtain a good exposure automatically, or with a manual camera, by simply setting the exposure the camera recommends. More than likely, though, your work won't conform to this tonal model. The solution to this problem is to show the camera's meter what it wants to see. You can do this with something called, rather simply, a "gray card," an 8″ × 10″ sheet of smooth, even gray cardboard manufactured by Kodak and other makers specifically for taking light readings. You can buy a package of two or three (they get smudged) for a few dollars in professional photography stores. The card reflects 18 percent of the light that strikes it, which is exactly the amount your camera assumes its subject reflects. The procedures described in later sections on lighting and determining exposure assume that you are using a gray card, so buy one when you pick up your film and lights.

The use of the card will be explained in more detail in later sections. Basically, once you've set up your lights, you simply place the card in the same light that falls on your artwork—against a piece of sculpture, or in the same plane as a painting or work on paper—and fill the camera's viewfinder with it. There's no need to focus the camera on the card, but you may want to secure the card in some way so that you have both hands free to operate the camera. Be sure not to cast a shadow on the card, nor to angle it in such a way that you pick up glare from your lights.

When you point it at the gray card, your camera will indicate a combination of aperture and shutter speed that will produce a correct exposure on the film. Remember that you can obtain correct exposure with various combinations; the most suitable combinations for each type of work and situation will be discussed later in this chapter and in the chapters on specific kinds of work. You will also learn how to override an automatic camera so that it will "remember" the correct exposure indicated by the gray card reading.

## FILM EXPOSURE AND EXPOSURE BRACKETING

If your camera is set to the correct ISO for the film you're using, its meter's "reading" of the light reflected by the gray card should tell you the correct exposure for your artwork. If, however, the artwork is especially light or dark, or high in contrast, it may make a better slide if slightly under- or overexposed. We'll see how to do this in a minute. But first, you should give a little thought to the best combination of shutter speed and aperture for your particular artwork. Remember that many such combinations will give you correct exposure. A gray card reading of 1/4 second at f8 will give you the same film exposure (i.e., lightness or darkness in the slide) as an exposure of 1/8 second at f5.6. This is because a one-stop decrease in the size of the lens opening—from f5.6 to f8—is exactly offset by a one-step slower shutter speed.

### CHOOSING A SHUTTER SPEED

Because you're using a tripod, you can select (within limits) as slow a shutter speed as you need without risking blur. Ordinarily, the strength of the lights you will be using, along with the smaller lens apertures (f-stops) that should be set when photographing artwork, will require that you use shutter speeds in the $^1/_{15}$ to one-second range. (This will vary according to the number and wattage of the lights you are using, how far from the work they are, and whether or not you are diffusing or bouncing them.)

One thing to keep in mind: The films you are using may undergo a loss of sensitivity at relatively slower shutter speeds, resulting in a darker slide than the same exposure would produce at a faster shutter speed. This phenomenon is called *reciprocity failure,* and the shutter speed at which it begins to happen depends on the film being used. (Of the recommended films, Ektachrome 50 and Fujichrome 64T are the least susceptible to this effect; Kodachrome KPA, on the other hand, shows some darkening at speeds slower than $^1/_8$ second.) But in general, the resulting underexposure can be compensated for by increasing your exposure by one-half to one stop, preferably by setting a wider lens aperture (increasing exposure by using slower shutter speeds will compound the effect), then "bracketing" your exposures on top of this. (Bracketing will be explained later in the chapter.) At very slow speeds, some films may also show color changes, so be wary. Reciprocity failure is usually more of an issue in photographing three-dimensional work, and you will be reminded about it in that section.

## CHOOSING AN APERTURE

The option to choose slower shutter speeds is important because you should use a relatively small aperture (higher-numbered f-stop) when photographing artwork. The size of the lens aperture affects something called *depth of field,* which, simply put, is the zone of sharpness in your subject on either side of your focused distance. The use of smaller apertures increases

the size of this zone, and becomes especially important in photographing three-dimensional work, or any other three-dimensional subject in which you want maximum clarity. And because a standard lens (unlike a macro lens) focuses on a curve, and not the flat plane formed by two-dimensional work, it's important in shooting flat artwork to have enough depth of field to compensate for the difference between the two.

The most useful tool in calculating depth of field at a given f-stop is the scale on the lens barrel. Its use is explained fully in the box on pages 34 and 35. Later sections will refer you back to this explanation.

The amount of depth of field you get at a *given* f-stop also varies considerably with the distance you've focused on. The closer you are to your subject—that is, the closer you've focused—the shallower your depth of field will be at a given aperture. For this reason, the smaller your artwork, the smaller the aperture you will need to set. Try to use an f-stop of f11, for example, if your flat work is less than two feet across. (If it's in the $8 \times 10$-inch range, try to shoot at f16.) Flat work larger than two feet across can be photographed at an aperture of f8, provided you focus carefully. Three-dimensional work, on the other hand, requires the use of even smaller f-stops than flat work, small enough to create a zone of sharpness adequate to encompass the entire depth of the work. Use the depth of field scale to determine which f-stop will do this. Very small three-dimensional works may even require f-stops as small as f22. However, the smallest aperture some lenses offer is f16. By contrast, macro lenses, because they are designed to focus as close as several inches, usually stop down to an aperture of

f32, but this is rarely necessary.

Whether two- or three-dimensional, the larger the artwork, the wider the aperture you can get away with, because larger works must be photographed from greater distances to keep them within the frame, and this increased distance improves depth of field. But avoid apertures wider than f5.6 if at all possible, or you may run a serious risk of having part of the work out of focus. And if you're using a lens or zoom focal length longer than 50- or 55mm, such as 85- or 105mm, use an aperture a stop smaller than those recommended above—for instance, f11 instead of f8. These recommendations are only general guidelines, and should be checked against the depth of field scale whenever possible. They may be particularly useful, though, for those using zoom lenses with skimpy depth of field scales.

Remember that you can set the lens aperture ring to in-between positions, too—for example, a half or a third of the way between f8 or f11. Depth of field at these settings can be determined by reading the distances "between the lines" on the depth of field scale. Again, the gray card reading should indicate the correct shutter speed at any chosen aperture. With a shutter-priority automatic camera, you can make the camera select a smaller aperture by setting a slower shutter speed.

## DEPTH OF FIELD AND THE VIEWFINDER IMAGE

It should be said that the appearance of any subject in your SLR camera's viewfinder is misleading in terms of depth of field. This is because, even though you may have set a small aperture like f11 on your lens, the camera keeps the aperture diaphragm open to its

## READING THE DEPTH OF FIELD SCALE ON YOUR LENS

Calculating *depth of field*—the depth of the zone of sharpness in your photograph—needn't be a seat-of-the-pants affair. Your camera's lens barrel is marked in such a way as to show you quite precisely how much of your subject will be clear in your final slide or print.

- *Aperture Ring.* The lens aperture is usually set with the ring on the lens barrel closest to the camera body. Most standard lenses such as the 50mm you are probably using have apertures ranging from f1.7, f1.8, or f2 down to f16 or f22; other lenses, particularly zooms, telephotos, and macro lenses, may have smaller maximum apertures such as f2.8, f3.5, or even f4. Macro lenses and long zooms or telephotos may stop down to an aperture as small as f32 or f45. On occasions when even apertures as small as f11 or f16 may not provide adequate depth of field, such as in shooting extreme close-ups, these smaller apertures may be useful. To select a particular aperture, you usually click it into place below a centered dot.
- *Focusing ring.* The next moving ring on your lens barrel is the focusing ring, which is engraved with scales in both meters and feet. (Be sure you don't confuse them.) When you focus on a subject, the number that represents its distance from the camera lines up with the engraved line centered on the lens barrel below it. (This mark is also aligned with the dot that indicates the aperture being used.) On either side of this line are more lines, each with a number engraved beneath or beside it. Notice that these lines refer to lens apertures, and that each number appears on both sides of the focusing mark. These lines are the depth-of-field scale.
- *Zone of Sharpness.* After you focus a subject, find the lines that correspond to your chosen aperture. These lines will indicate two distances on the focusing ring, to either side of your focused distance. This is the range within which your subject will be sharp.

For example, say your subject is seven feet away; you focus on it, and the number 7 on the foot scale lines up with the engraved mark. The lines marked 8 on the depth-of-field scale fall at six feet on the right and around nine feet on the left. This means that at an aperture of f8, your zone of sharpness will run from six to nine feet when you're focused at seven feet. Note how depth of field improves if you choose to set your aperture at f16; the zone of sharpness extends from about five feet to twelve feet.

On certain camera lenses, most notably those made by Nikon, the manufacturer has simply color-coded the lines on the depth of field scale to match the colors of the actual aperture numbers, thus eliminating the need for more engraved numbers. For example, f11 on the aperture ring is yellow, and the lines on the depth of field scale that show you the zone of sharpness at f11 are also yellow.

You may notice that your focused distance also has an effect on depth of field. In the example above, with the aperture set at f8,

focusing ring

distance

depth of field scale

aperture ring

widest setting until just before you trip the shutter, when it automatically stops it down. It does this to allow as much light as possible into the viewfinder, to provide a bright image for framing and focusing. But this also means that the depth of field of any given subject as observed through the lens is that available at its widest aperture, and therefore much shallower than what you'll get when the lens is stopped down to your selected aperture before the shutter is tripped.

Many SLRs offer a control called the "depth-of-field preview button," which allows you to view your subject through the lens at the f-stop you've set. Unless you've set your lens to its widest aperture (lowest f-number), this will cause the viewfinder image of your subject to darken—in fact, the smaller the aperture you set, the darker it will be. This darkening makes such visual judgment of depth of field very unreliable. It's better to make use of the lens' depth of field scale, and focus the lens to maximize depth of field, as explained in the box. The viewfinder image produced by your lens' maximum aperture may be disconcerting if you're shooting three-dimensional work, because parts of the artwork will appear to be unsharp. Just remember, though, that the photograph will be taken through the smaller aperture you have set, and thus show considerably better depth of field.

Once you've set a manual camera or a camera in a manual mode to the appropriate combination of aperture and shutter speed, using the gray card to guide you, it will remain at those settings until you change them yourself. When you remount your camera on the tripod, the camera may recommend a different exposure based on its

focusing on fifteen feet instead of seven would give you a zone of sharpness from ten feet to about twenty-five feet, much deeper than the three-foot zone you would get when focused at seven feet. In fact, the closer you focus, the shallower your depth of field will be at a given aperture, which is why smaller artworks require the use of smaller lens apertures, especially if they're three-dimensional.

- *In Focus.* Depth of field at any given aperture can and should be maximized by careful focusing. With two-dimensional artwork, it's safest to focus on the middle of the piece, then select a moderately small aperture to deepen the zone of sharpness in compensation for the fact that most lenses focus on a curve, not the flat plane formed by two-dimensional artwork. Specific apertures will be discussed in chapter 3. With three-dimensional work and installation views, focusing on the closest part of your subject wastes the available depth of field in front of your focused distance. Depth of field at any aperture extends about twice as far behind where you've focused as it does in front of it, which means that if you focus a third of the way between the nearest thing that must be sharp and the farthest thing, then choose an aperture that provides a deep enough zone of sharpness to include them both, you'll be getting the most out of any given aperture's depth of field. This strategy will be reiterated in the sections on three-dimensional work and installation views.

## EXPOSURE COMPENSATION DIAL

Often found around the rewind crank of automatic cameras, this dial is marked in stops— +1, -1, +2, -2—each of which is equivalent to a one-step change in aperture or shutter speed.

averaged reading of the artwork's tones. Ignore these readings and take your pictures.

## FILM EXPOSURE WITH AN AUTOMATIC CAMERA

If your camera offers automatic exposure only, the exposure it will choose when you put your camera back on the tripod and make the artwork fill the frame probably won't agree with the gray card reading. If it does agree, you can let the camera do its automatic thing; if it doesn't, you will need to override the camera's choice in some way. (If the automatic reading off the artwork itself is only slightly different than the gray card reading, and your camera has an exposure compensation dial, you can simply *bracket* the automatic exposure enough to include the ex-

posure indicated by the gray card reading, a technique explained later.)

**Exposure Compensation Dial.** If you're not sure what, if any, exposure override controls your camera offers, check the manual. The most common is an *exposure compensation* dial, often found around the rewind crank along with the ISO setting. The dial is marked in stops— +1, -1, +2, -2—each of which is the equivalent of a one-step change in aperture or shutter speed. Usually the in-between positions are marked in thirds. Setting the exposure compensation dial to + 2/3, for example, will give the film an additional 2/3 stop of exposure, making your slide lighter than it would have been had you let the camera use the exposure it had indicated. Setting the dial to -2, on the other hand, will give the film two stops less exposure, making the slide considerably darker than it would have been.

In order to get your automatic camera, with the artwork filling its viewfinder, to give the film the exposure that the gray card reading indicated, simply turn the exposure compensation dial until the exposure indicated in the viewfinder display matches the gray card reading you took in the center of the artwork. For example, say you got a reading of 1/4 second at halfway between f8 and f11 with your shutter-priority automatic. When you remount your camera so that the artwork fills the frame, the camera indicates f16—a smaller aperture which will produce less exposure than the artwork really needs. Leaving the shutter speed set the same, turn the exposure compensation dial toward the plus side, until the aperture indicated in the viewfinder display is between f8 and f11, as it was with the card reading. If you look at the dial, it

will be halfway between +1 and +2. This kind of correction is more likely with an artwork that is, on average, lighter in tone than the gray card.

If a work is darker in tone than the card, you will probably have to make a correction in the opposite direction, because automatic exposure systems tend to overexpose very dark subjects. If the gray card reading was 1/2 second at f8, but the work itself causes the camera to choose 1/2 second at f5.6, turn the exposure compensation dial toward the minus side, until the aperture display reads f8. The exposure compensation dial will then read -1.

If your automatic camera is an aperture-priority model, you will have to use the shutter speed the gray card reading indicated at your selected aperture as the "target" for your exposure-compensation dial adjustments. If, for example, with the aperture set at f11 the gray card reading caused the camera to choose 1/4 second, but the camera's reading off the work itself indicates 1/8 second, set the exposure compensation dial to +1, to obtain the additional stop of exposure. The viewfinder's shutter-speed display should then indicate 1/4 second. If the reading off the work itself indicates that the camera will choose a shutter speed of one second, which would result in severe overexposure of the work, set the exposure compensation dial at -2, which should cause the viewfinder to display 1/4 second.

As mentioned, the exposure compensation control is usually located around the rewind crank, and is an integral part of the ISO dial. In fact, the exposure compensation dial actually changes the ISO setting (internally) to override the camera's automatic exposure system. If your camera has no exposure override mechanism, you can resort to changing the ISO setting to obtain the correct exposure. Turn it as described above, until the viewfinder display you get when the camera is reading off the artwork itself matches your gray card reading. Turn it toward the higher numbers to reduce exposure; this makes the meter think the film is more sensitive to light than it really is, so it gives it less exposure. This is the usual correction for an artwork that is dark. Turn the ISO dial toward the lower numbers to increase exposure; this makes the meter think the film is less sensitive than it really is, so it gives it more exposure. If your camera sets the ISO only automatically by reading a "DX" code on the side of the film cartridge, you can't use this technique.

**Exposure lock.** Another automatic exposure override system common on more sophisticated cameras is the *autoexposure lock* or *memory*. This is usually a button on the front of the camera that you hold in after taking your local reading—in our case, off the gray card. Holding the button in locks in the setting, preventing the camera from recalculating the exposure (incorrectly) when you show it the whole subject—in our case, the artwork. The problem with this device is that you usually have to keep depressing the button until you make the exposure, awkward if you must then remount the camera on the tripod. Furthermore, it's not a good idea to have any hand contact with the camera when you're using the longer shutter speeds necessary in tungsten light. But if the design of the exposure lock on your camera doesn't present any of these problems, simply take your reading off the gray card, lock the exposure in, remount the camera, and take your

pictures. Be sure that the exposure remains locked in if you're bracketing your exposures.

## MAKING AND BRACKETING YOUR EXPOSURES

Once you've established the correct exposure for your combination of film speed and lighting, and chosen and set a suitable combination of aperture and shutter speed (and if necessary, figured out how to trick your camera into using this combination), you're finally ready to take your long-awaited photographs. Make sure you've focused properly, that the artwork is square and/or centered in the viewfinder (the fine points are treated in the next two chapters), and that all extraneous light sources have been eliminated. Don't forget that you must use a cable release to trip the shutter, to eliminate camera movement during long exposures.

After you've exposed your first frame, advance the film slowly and gently. Don't force the film advance lever any further than it needs to go to move to the next frame. Too much pressure may cause the camera to shift on the mounting screw. Keep double-checking the viewfinder as you expose more frames to be sure that this hasn't happened. Most cameras will allow you to advance the film in several short strokes rather than a single long one, which can be useful in preventing this problem. Before making the next exposure, allow ten seconds or more for any vibrations caused by advancing the film to stop. If you live over a subway or a factory, make your exposures when the train has passed or the machines are quiet. Vibrations can be transmitted right through the tripod.

Shoot as many slides at your

chosen exposure as you think you will need. You can always use the extras, and a good original slide is better in quality than a commercial duplicate. It's cheaper, too.

In spite of everything you've done to assure proper exposure of your film, you should still *bracket* your exposures (on the other hand, many professionals are so familiar with their meterings that they don't bracket)—that is, shoot additional "insurance" frames with both more and less exposure than that indicated by the final gray card reading. Photographic film is at best an unpredictable material, and even if given precisely the exposure that is recommended for it, it may yield a result that is a little too light or dark. In particular, a light artwork may look better in a slide if it is slightly underexposed; a very dark artwork may look better if somewhat overexposed. And you may choose to make your slides a little lighter or darker depending on the circumstances in which they will be viewed: a darker slide for projection, a lighter one for viewing in frosted slide pages. It should be said, though, that variations that are noticeable in a slide aren't usually significant in a negative that you intend to have printed, and can be adjusted for when the print is made.

## BRACKETING EXPOSURES WITH A MANUAL CAMERA

Bracketing your exposures is easy with a manual camera, or a camera in a manual mode. If your indicated exposure is ¼ second at f11, for example, shoot a frame at ¼ second with the aperture set halfway between f8 and f11, then another with it set halfway between f11 and f16. The first will give you a slide that is slightly lighter than the one your calculated exposure will yield; the second, a slide that is slightly darker. This is called bracketing by a half-stop. If your calculated exposure called for the aperture to be set between f8 and f11, you would bracket a half-stop in either direction by taking a second picture with the aperture set at f8 and a third with it set at f11. You can extrapolate a half-stop bracket from any in-between setting, for that matter. As you get more confident, you can also bracket by thirds of a stop, setting the aperture a third of the way from f11 to f8, then a third of the way from f11 to f16. Even this small change will produce noticeably different slides, but often the calculated exposure and one or more brackets will produce slides that are acceptable.

You can bracket even further on either side of your indicated exposure if you think your work may not be typical. In the example described above, you might shoot additional brackets a full stop over—at f8—and a full stop under, at f16. If you're bracketing in thirds of stops, shoot frames at ⅔ over—i.e., at ⅔ of the way from f11 to f8—and ⅔ under, at ⅔ of the way from f11 to f16. If you want to save film by eliminating one of these broader brackets, go with ⅔ or one stop over for dark work, ⅔ or one stop under for light work, eliminating the bracket at the other extreme.

**Shutter Speed.** You can also use variations in shutter speed to bracket exposures. You may opt to do this when you're afraid that using a wider aperture to bracket your exposure might compromise your depth of field. (There's little harm in using a smaller f-stop to bracket on the "underexposure" side, because it can only improve your depth of field.) In the example above, for instance, if you were reluctant to open the lens aperture all the way to f8 to obtain a stop of extra exposure, you could use a one-

stop slower shutter speed—½ second instead of ¼—to obtain the same result. If you wanted to bracket a half-stop over without opening the lens aperture to a setting halfway between f8 and f11, you could also change the shutter speed to ½ second. This in effect increases exposure by a whole stop, so if you close the lens aperture down a half-stop, to between f11 and f16, you reduce the whole stop increase to a half.

As a rule, shoot as many frames on each bracket as you think you will need final slides, until you become more experienced, and get a sense of what the acceptable exposure range for your work is.

## BRACKETING EXPOSURES WITH AN AUTOMATIC CAMERA

If you're working with an automatic camera, use the exposure compensation dial to bracket your exposures. If it's set at 0, bracket in halves or thirds in either direction, by setting the dial at +½ or +⅓, +1 or +⅔, -½ or -⅓, and -1 or -⅔. If you've already adjusted the exposure compensation dial to match your gray card reading, use its adjusted position as a starting point. For example, if your exposure compensation dial is already set at +1, make exposures at +1½ or +1⅓, +2 or +1⅔, then +½ or +⅔, 0 or +⅓.

**ISO.** If your camera offers no exposure compensation control, you'll have to use the film-speed (ISO) dial to alter exposure. The half-stop changes described above can be achieved either by increasing the ISO number by roughly 50 percent, which will cause the camera to give the film a half-stop less exposure, or decreasing the ISO number by 25 percent, which will cause the camera to give the film a half-stop more exposure. One-third stop changes can be obtained

by increasing the ISO number by one notch on the dial, which will cause the camera to give the film a third-stop less exposure (the equivalent of -⅓ on an exposure compensation control), or reducing it by a notch, which will cause the camera to give the film a third-stop more exposure. If the exact ISO that you need isn't marked, set the nearest number. If you've already adjusted the ISO setting to make the camera's automatic exposure system's reading of your artwork match the gray card reading, use that adjusted ISO as a starting point.

As you become more familiar with the way photographic film records your artwork, you can be more parsimonious in your bracketing. If you find, for instance, that the best slide always seems to be either the one indicated by the gray card reading, or the one a half-stop less exposed than it, then you can limit yourself to those two, shooting as many frames on each as you will need slides. This presumes, however, that your work is fairly consistent in tonality.

In the abstract, all this information may seem a bit overwhelming. But it will make much more sense when you're shooting your work, and when you see your first results. You will, however, have to make some initial decisions about film and lights; if you can afford to experiment, do so.

Techniques that relate specifically to different kinds of work are presented in the following two chapters. If your work is two-dimensional, read Chapter Three; if it's three-dimensional, read Chapter Four. You might want to skim the chapter that doesn't pertain to your work, just for the extra insight it may provide. Good luck!

# SUMMARY/ **SEEING THE LIGHT: THE BASICS**

- In photography, light is described by its color temperature. Daylight has a different color temperature than artificial light.
- Films are designed (balanced) to be used with a specific color temperature of light. They produce accurate color only in the kind of light they are balanced for.
- Tungsten light and tungsten-balanced slide films are best for photographing works of art because they offer greater control.
- Tungsten lamps are available in color temperatures of 3400 degrees Kelvin for tungsten Kodachrome (KPA) and 3200 degrees Kelvin for tungsten Ektachrome films.
- The higher the film's ISO number, the greater its sensitivity to light, or speed.
- Films with low ISO numbers are good for photographing art because they produce a sharp, fine-grained image of the work.
- "Professional" films are designed for critical use, such as photographing artwork, and must be stored in a refrigerator. Allow them to warm up before using them, and return them to the refrigerator if you don't plan to have them processed immediately.
- Ektachrome films can be processed by a professional lab or independent photofinisher; Kodachrome must be sent to a special processing facility.
- Tungsten photofloods are available in two profiles: a standard, lightbulb-shaped lamp, which must be used with a metal reflector, and a reflector photoflood lamp.
- 500-watt lamps are usually needed for all but the smallest artwork. Color-rated photofloods must be burned conservatively, and a record kept of how long they're on.
- In a pinch, you can use regular, high-wattage lightbulbs and High-Speed "amateur" tungsten Ektachrome to photograph your artwork.
- The 81A filter is useful in eliminating the blue cast that can turn up in even the most carefully made slide.
- Eliminate all other sources of light when using tungsten light to photograph your artwork.
- A film of a given ISO needs to receive a specific amount of light to produce an acceptable exposure. The shutter speed (length of exposure) and lens aperture (f-stop) allow you to regulate the light to obtain this quantity.
- The relationship between shutter speed and lens aperture is proportional: a one-stop smaller aperture can be compensated for by using a one-step slower shutter speed (i.e., an increase in exposure time), to produce the same exposure.
- Since a camera's meter assumes that all the tones in an artwork (or any subject) will average out to a specific medium gray, the meter may miscalculate an incorrect combination of f-stop and shutter speed.
- Take the light reading off an 18 percent gray card to give the meter the tone it is calibrated for, resulting in a consistently correct exposure.
- Because it keeps the camera steady, a tripod permits the longer shutter speeds required in photographing artwork, usually 1/15 to one second.
- Depth of field—the depth of the zone of sharpness in your photograph—is increased by using smaller f-stops.
- Because of its greater depth, three-dimensional artwork requires the use of smaller lens apertures than two-dimensional work. The smaller the artwork, the smaller the f-stop you must use to photograph it.
- If an automatic exposure system's averaged light reading of your artwork disagrees with the gray card reading, adjust the camera's exposure compensation dial, if it has one, to make it match.
- The camera's ISO dial may also be used as an exposure override mechanism. Setting lower numbers than the ISO recommended for the film will increase film exposure; setting higher numbers will reduce exposure.
- When you make your exposures, keep checking the camera's viewfinder to make sure the camera hasn't shifted on its mounting screw.
- Advance the film gently, and allow time for vibrations to subside before exposing the next frame.
- Shoot as many slides at your chosen exposure as you think you will need final slides. Shoot the same number on each exposure bracket.
- Bracket your exposure generously in your first attempts at photographing your work; as you begin to see a pattern in the exposures that are best for your work, you can limit the bracketing range.

If you're a painter who goes to great pains to make your stretchers square, you've doubtless been disappointed when the slides you've shot of your work represent it as a trapezoid, a rhombus, or any other kind of quadrilateral. This happens when you don't take care to make the sides of the artwork parallel to the edges of the camera's viewfinder before you take the photograph. This not only distorts the shape of the work, but distracts from its content, particularly if it's strongly graphic or rectilinear. The camera adjustments that correct this condition aren't instinctive, yet without them, squaring up the work becomes a trial-and-error chore. If the few simple procedures outlined here are followed, you'll save yourself a lot of aggravation.

## SETTING UP

Place your work on a secure surface. If you can't hang a painting on the wall, place it on an easel or a shelf if it's small enough, or rest it on the floor against a wall if it's large. If it's a vertical piece, put it on its side. Works on paper, such as prints and drawings, can be attached to the wall with strong tape on the back of the work, or with pushpins if you can accept their encroachments as part of the presentation of the piece. Just be sure to position the work so that you can operate the camera at a comfortable height. If you're resting the work on the floor or a shelf, angle it up slightly to accomplish this (which you will have to do anyway to make it stand). Make sure there's enough room in front of the piece for the tripod and you— scope it out with the camera if you're uncertain—and to the sides

of it for the lights. The larger the work, the more room you'll need both ways.

**Positioning the Tripod.** Once the artwork is in place, follow these steps to position your camera and tripod: By looking through the camera, determine about how far from the work the tripod should be placed. Set up the tripod there, making sure to extend the legs evenly so that its sliding post is plumb. For greater stability, extend the upper, thicker leg sections of the tripod first, to their fullest position. If you need to extend a portion of the lower sections, it's easier to do so before spreading the tripod legs, because you can measure each leg against the others for evenness. Lock in each section securely with the locking nut or clamp.

At the same time, extend the sliding post several inches, to allow for future lowering adjustments, and lock it in securely. The combined height of the legs and post should place the camera on an imaginary line running out from the center of the artwork and perpendicular to it.

**Camera Angle.** Mount the camera on the tripod head, so that it is parallel to the side lever and at a right angle to the forward-backward tilt of the head. Be sure that the camera is secure enough so that it won't twist on the mounting screw when you advance the film.

If the artwork is leaning back against a wall, use the tripod's rear adjusting arm to incline the camera forward at approximately the same angle. If the work is on a vertical wall, adjust the camera to a vertical position. A carpenter's angle finder or a bubble level is useful for these adjustments. The level should

have a bubble tube running perpendicular to the length of the level itself. (If the tilt of the artwork is steep, however, a level may not be reliable.) Place the level or angle finder against the surface of the artwork, and note the position of the bubble or needle. Then place it flat against the camera back, or if protrusions interfere, against the end of the lens barrel. Then adjust the camera's tilt until the reading matches that taken against the artwork.

**Fine Tuning.** Finally, adjust your distance from the work by moving the whole tripod forward or backward. Refocus the lens as you do, because focus can have a small effect on the size of the viewfinder image of the artwork.

The artwork should fill the viewfinder frame, but because the slide mount (and usually a commercial color or black and white print) will crop out a small amount of the image area on all sides, leave a small margin, perhaps 5 percent of each dimension. (See box on page 43.) Remember to adjust for any discrepancies between your viewfinder and what ends up on film, as discussed earlier. This will vary from camera to camera. If your camera shifts the image to the right, frame up your work off-center a like amount to the left, and maintain it in this position as you square the work up. If your viewfinder shows you a lot less than you will get on film, allow less space between the edges of the artwork and the sides of the viewfinder.

## CAMERA ANGLE

If the artwork is leaning back against the wall, use the tripod's rear adjusting arm to incline the camera forward at the same angle. Use a bubble level if necessary to adjust so the film is exactly parallel to the artwork.

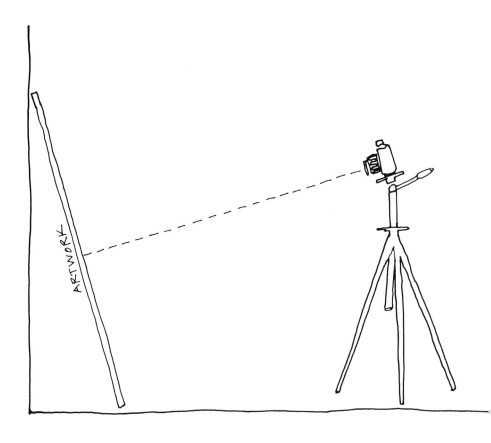

## SQUARING UP

The procedure of squaring up your artwork is in essence a way of making sure that the film is parallel to the surface of the artwork when you photograph it. This is the only way that its true shape—whether perfectly square or not—can be recorded. Although you haven't set up your lights yet, you may want to throw some extra light on your artwork so you'll have a bright viewfinder image to work with.

## SPECIFIC PROBLEMS—AND SOLUTIONS

As you look through the camera, you'll probably see that the image of the artwork is skewed. Examine it carefully, using the edges of the viewfinder as a reference. *If the artwork is narrower at the top than the bottom*—that is, the sides taper toward the top—unlock the rear tripod arm and tilt the camera forward until the right and left sides seem parallel to the sides of the viewfinder, then lock the tripod head with the arm or its separate locking nut. This adjustment, which in effect enlarges the top edge of the work, will begin to crop into the top edge and push the bottom edge well into the frame. In order to correct this, loosen the center column and raise it, keeping the work centered, until you've brought the top edge back into the viewfinder. Raise it until the artwork is centered again.

*If the artwork is narrower at the bottom than at the top,* tilt the camera backward until the sides are parallel. (Basic geometry: in a rectangle, if the left and right sides are parallel, the length of the top and bottom will be the same.) This will cause the work to drop in the viewfinder, so loosen the column and lower it to re-center the work. This is why you need to extend the column initially, because if you try to lower the camera by shortening the tripod legs, you will probably undo your hard-won parallelism.

*Apply the same technique if the top and bottom of the work converge to either side.* If they converge to the right—that is, the right side of the work appears shorter than the left—loosen the head-locking nut and rotate the camera to the left until they are parallel. (Do not loosen the column to rotate the tripod head.) The image of the artwork will then shift to the right in the viewfinder frame, and you will

# FRAMING UP YOUR WORK: THE FINER POINTS

Unless you're a photorealist whose work conforms to the image area of a 35mm camera, your painting, print, or other work will rarely fit precisely into the viewfinder. In fact, the more square the piece is, the more studio clutter or spackled wallboard will end up in the frame. There are two solutions to this problem. One is to cover the wall behind the piece with black paper or cloth, although when the slide is projected some light will inevitably get through it and reveal its texture. Black velvet, velour, or velveteen are best for this purpose because they are so nonreflective. But a better solution is to block out the offending areas on the finished slide itself with a special slide-masking tape, which will be described in chapter 7. Likewise, a photographic print can be cropped by a lab or trimmed at a later stage.

- *On the Edge.* If you're photographing a work on paper, it's often important to show the edge of the sheet, especially if it's a water-color or print with a deckled edge. In this case, you should back the work with a contrasting material, dark if the work is light in tone, light if it's dark. If the proportions of your work are such that this leaves large areas of the material to either side of the piece, you can mask the slide with tape to match the margin at the long edges of the opening in the slide, where the edge of the work comes closest.

  Anytime you want to be sure the edges of a work are visible, or if you want a white border in a slide of a matted work to show that it's matted, leave a little extra room around it when you size it up in the viewfinder. In any and all cases, be sure the artwork is centered in the viewfinder, with equal amounts of space on either side. (If your camera shifts the image to the side, however, you will need to compensate for this by framing the work off-center.) Inconsistently off-center slides can be disconcerting when projected, because the image jumps back and forth on the screen.

- *Dark Work.* The squaring-up procedure described here assumes that your artwork is reasonably square, and depends on your being able to discern clearly the edges of the work. Even if you've thrown a lot of light on the work, if its tones are predominantly dark and you've backed it with black paper or cloth, you may have trouble seeing the edges. To make it easier to spot them, put sheets of white paper behind or abutting the work, and remove them when you're ready to shoot. Or simply wait until you're about to shoot and slip your black cloth or paper behind the piece. In either case, be very careful not to disturb the position of the piece.

- *Light Work.* If a work is very light in tone and you're photographing it against a light wall (and intend to mask the slide), you may find it easier to discern the edges if you slip a few sheets of black paper behind the piece.

have to move the whole tripod very carefully to the right so as not to disrupt the parallelism of the top and bottom of the work.

If the top and bottom of the artwork converge to the left—that is, the left side appears shorter than the right—rotate the camera to the right until they are parallel, then shift the tripod to the left to center the work in the frame again.

If shifting the tripod laterally disrupts the parallelism of the top and bottom of the work, repeat the squaring procedure in the new position. Alternate this technique for the sides and then the top and bottom, and repeat it until the work is square and centered.

*If the sides or the top and bottom of your artwork appear parallel but "lean" one way or the other,* loosen the side arm of the tripod head and tilt the camera sideways to correct it. This may reveal that the edges of the work aren't really parallel to the sides of the viewfinder, so repeat the squaring procedure again. Manipulate the side tilt frequently as you square up, using the edge of the viewfinder frame as a reference. You can also use a bubble level on the top of the work and camera, if the camera has a flat portion to rest it on.

If your camera is not oriented vertically—that is, if the artwork is leaning back against the wall—it's better to make any small rotational adjustments by loosening the tripod's mounting screw and twisting the camera on it. This is because rotation of the tripod head itself will not maintain the proper orientation of film plane to subject plane. However, rotating the camera on the platform itself changes its relationship to the side tilt and forward-backward tilt levers, which could complicate further squaring-up procedures, so make an effort to center the camera laterally early

Right.

Wrong.

in the process.

Squaring up takes practice, and even an experienced person can get bogged down and frustrated. If the procedure seems to be going nowhere, kick the tripod out of whack (not out of frustration) and start fresh.

**If Your Work Isn't Square.** If your artwork isn't square nor meant to be, if it's a circle or a triangle or an amoeba shape, the technique described above obviously can't be used. In this event, you should square up on a rectangular work of the same size and simply replace it with the odd-shaped work, making sure that the latter is in the same plane and position as its proxy. If a rectangular work isn't available, cut a rectangular piece of cardboard or paper with the same approximate dimensions (circumference, in the case of a circular work) and square up on it. This is the only way to be sure that the shape of the work in the photograph will correspond exactly to the original.

## LENSES AND TWO-DIMENSIONAL WORK

Squaring up can be somewhat easier with a "longer" focal length lens, such as a 90mm or 105mm telephoto. But even if you have access to such a lens, you may be constrained from using it by the size of the space you're working in. Like a telescope, a long lens has a relatively narrow angle of view, which requires that you be farther from the work to fit it into the camera's viewfinder. If your space is small, if your work is large, or both, you may not be able to use it. On the other hand, the closest focusing distance of a long lens may place you too far away from a small artwork to fill the frame with it. Some newer zoom lenses offer a

"macro" mode, which will allow you to focus closely, down to as little as half a foot from your subject. These lenses are a viable alternative to macro lenses and close-up attachments, and you may find them indispensable if your artwork is small. It's especially important, though, to select smaller lens apertures if you are using a long lens or a zoom set to macro mode to shoot small work. Refer to the section on shooting very small work, page 96, for further information.

### WIDE-ANGLE LENSES

On the other extreme, if your work is very large relative to your working space, you may find that the standard 50mm or 55mm lens doesn't encompass its entire surface even when your tripod's against the far wall. In this case, you either have to relocate to a larger space, or use a slightly wide-angle lens such as a 35mm, which will allow you to include more of the work from the same distance. ("35mm" here is a reference to the lens' focal length, not to the 35mm film format of the camera itself.) The price of this advantage is some distortion. The center of the work may appear to bulge, and with even wider-angle lenses such as 28- or 24mm, the sides may appear to bow out. Wide-angle lenses make squaring up the work much more difficult; avoid using them if at all possible.

Most fixed lenses on automatic 35mm compact non-SLR cameras are moderately wide-angle, usually from 35- to 40mm in focal length. They will inevitably distort the work to some extent, although not as badly as the image in the viewfinder might suggest. You can minimize the distortion caused by a wide-angle lens by moving farther away from the work, but this will, of course, reduce the size of the work on the resulting film. If you're

If the artwork converges toward the top,

tilt the camera forward until the sides are parallel.

Then raise the column to center the work.

If the artwork converges toward the bottom,

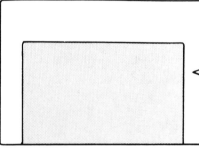

tilt the camera backward until the sides are parallel.

Then lower the column to center the work.

If the artwork converges toward the right,

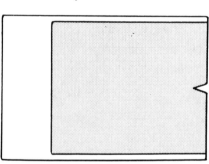

rotate the camera to the left until the top and bottom are parallel.

Then move the tripod to the right to center the work.

If the artwork converges toward the left,

rotate the camera to the right until the top and bottom are parallel.

Then move the tripod to the left to center the work.

shooting slides, this is probably unacceptable; if you're shooting film for the sole purpose of making prints, you can have a custom lab enlarge and crop the image to size, or have a commercial photo finisher make a print a size larger than you need, then trim it.

A zoom lens of moderately wide-angle to medium-telephoto range—for example, 28-80 or 35-70—may bail you out in the kind of tight shooting situation that a 50mm lens is too "long" for. Setting it in the 40-odd-mm range will allow you to include more of the work without the distortion likely from a 35mm lens, which is the nearest wide-angle alternative in a lens of fixed focal length. Always use the lens at its longest possible setting to minimize distortion; in other words, get as far away from the artwork as possible, then adjust the zoom setting to make the artwork fill the frame. If space allows, you should certainly use such a lens at its 50mm setting, or beyond.

## SHOOTING MORE THAN ONE WORK

If you're shooting more than one artwork, particularly if the pieces are of similar size, you can expedite the framing and squaring-up procedure by using pieces of masking tape as register marks. If you're leaning a painting against a wall, for example, put an "L" of masking tape at the lower corners; if you've hung or taped the work on the wall, put tape marks at all corners. Even if the second piece you plan to photograph isn't the same width, these marks will help you center it, and if the work is more or less the same height as the first, placing its bottom edge the same distance from the wall will maintain the same angle, eliminating the need to square it up again.

## SHOOTING DETAILS

Sometimes an overall view of a work fails to convey its full richness, especially if it is never projected or enlarged. If your work is large and/or complex, or if it has distinctive surface characteristics, you should consider shooting details of it to supplement the overall view. If you're not using a macro lens, or a zoom lens with a "macro" mode, shooting details often requires the use of close-up attachments. Read the section concerning small work on page 96 for more details.

Because depth of field is reduced at the close distances involved in shooting details, you should use smaller lens f-stops. This will in turn require the use of slower shutter speeds to obtain equivalent exposure. If you boost the light levels, however, you may be able to use smaller apertures without changing shutter speeds. Anytime you change the light, of course (whether to brighten the artwork or alter the light's character and direction to suit a specific detail), you will have to take a new meter reading and change your camera's settings accordingly.

## LIGHTING TWO-DIMENSIONAL WORK

In photographing three-dimensional artwork, light has a descriptive function, defining surfaces and contours by causing the work to cast shadows on itself. By contrast, the primary function of lighting in photographing two-dimensional work is simply to ensure that the entire surface of the work receives the same amount of light, so that its tones and colors are reproduced in their true relationships.

If your work is heavily textured or impastoed, or includes areas of relief, you may want to light it as if it were sculptural, using a single

diffused source of light and reflectors to fill in shadows. Unfortunately, it is much harder to obtain even light across a broad surface using this technique, and you may run the risk of glare if you attempt to compensate for any unevenness by moving the light source so that it strikes the work at a more direct angle. You'll have to assess the trade-off in terms of the character of your specific work. But if you opt for the standard treatment described here, using direct light on either side of the work, be on the lookout for double shadows. These can, if necessary, be softened by diffusing or bouncing both light sources, as described in the section on lighting three-dimensional work in chapter 4.

## SETTING UP THE LIGHTS

For work of moderate to small size, two lamps of the 500-watt varieties described in chapter 2 are usually adequate. For large work, you may want to consider the use of four lamps, two on either side of the work in low and high positions. If your work is large and you only have two bulbs, place them far enough away to ensure that the light will fall evenly across the surface of the work. The disadvantage to this is that the intensity of the light drops off geometrically as you back the lamps away, requiring longer exposures (slower shutter speeds), and in some circumstances even the use of unacceptably wide lens apertures. A faster film, such as Kodak's High-Speed Tungsten Ektachrome, will make more efficient use of such lowered light levels.

**Placing the Light.** Once you've set up your tripod, camera, and artwork, it's easy to establish proper position for your lights. In essence, you want to light flat work at an angle from both sides. If you're using a single lamp on either side, each should be placed at a height corresponding to a point midway up the artwork. If the work is leaning back, then keep the lights at the level of the plane formed by the midline of the artwork and the camera position, angling them down slightly. If you're using two lamps on either side of the work, place the high ones at a level corresponding to a quarter of the way down from the top of the work, or higher, the low ones at a level corresponding to a quarter of the way up from the bottom of the work, or lower. The risk in using two lamps on either side is that you'll get a "hot" area in the horizontal center of the work, so you may find yourself raising or angling the upper bulbs up and lowering or angling the lower bulbs down a bit to avoid this.

Unless you've purchased photographic light stands, described in the "Useful Accessories" appendix, you'll have to improvise when it comes to securing your clip-on light fixtures. A painter's ladder can be used, as long as it's high enough; the back of a tall chair will suffice if the work is placed fairly low. Don't try to make up for placing a lamp at an incorrect height by angling it up or down. You'll risk uneven light.

**Preventing Flare.** As a general rule, keep the lights in the same plane as the camera—in other words, as far from the plane of the work (i.e., the wall you're working against) as the camera and tripod. If you place your lamps too far forward of the camera, direct light may strike the camera lens, causing *flare,* a fogging or veiling of the image, in your pictures. If you look back into the lens as you position your lights, you will be able to see any light falling directly across the lens surface.

If you feel you must place the

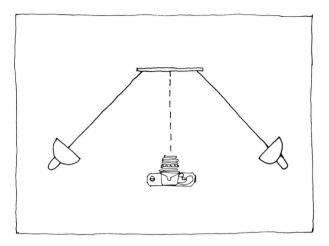

**LIGHTING SET-UP**
The angle and aim point of the lights can be varied to suit individual artworks, as described in the text, but be sure the lights aren't at such a steep angle that they cause glare on the sides of the work, or at such a shallow angle that the light is uneven. In general, lights should not be placed at an angle greater than 45 degrees from the wall.

lights forward of the camera, perhaps to maximize their effect on a larger work that has forced you to place the camera far away from it, you can prevent flare by *baffling* the lens. This may be done by taping small black cards to either side of the lens barrel, so that they extend far enough out from the front of the lens to block the light falling across its front element, or by setting up larger cards to either side of the camera, between it and the lights. A *lens hood,* a rubber or metal shade made for your specific lens, will also give you more flexibility in placing your lights. Independent manufacturers make clip-on or screw-in lens attachments for holding square gelatin filters, which usually have "barn door" flaps on either side to cut out stray light. However you deal with this problem, be sure that your baffle doesn't intrude into the picture area. Many macro lenses are designed with the front element considerably recessed, so that the lens barrel itself acts as a shade.

Lens hood.

Filter holder attachment with "barn doors."

**Preventing Glare.** The other general rule to placing your lights is to make sure the angle formed by the lights and the plane of the work (i.e., the wall, if you're shooting the work against one) is no greater than 45 degrees. If you place the lights closer to the camera position, so that they strike the work more directly, you may cause glare on the sides of the work.

With these general principles in mind, position one of the lights. Then using your foot as a ruler measure the distance between the light and the camera. Place the other light at the same distance from the camera, and at the same distance from the wall or the plane of work. If the angle of the lights is relatively steep—that is, close to 45 degrees—aim the lamps at the near side or center of the work. If the lights are closer to the plane of the work, striking it at a more oblique angle, aim them at the far edge of the work, to reduce the likelihood of having too much light on its sides.

Turn the lights on, and look through the camera. If any sign of glare is apparent on the sides of the work, move the lights closer to the wall so that they strike the work more obliquely. Don't make the angle any more oblique than necessary to eliminate the glare, because you may run the risk of uneven light, specifically of not enough light reaching the vertical middle of the work. To get a better sense of the angle at which glare begins to occur, stand right behind the camera with your eyes at the film plane, shifting your eyepoint laterally as you look at the side of the work opposite the direction your eyes are moving.

**Cover-Ups.** If there are any reflective or brightly colored surfaces near or adjacent to the work, it's advisable to cover them with cloth or paper of neutral tone, preferably gray or black. Depending on their angle relative to the lights and the artwork, they can contribute a color cast to parts of the work. If you are shooting a large work which is resting on a polyurethaned wooden floor, for example, light reflected off the floor may give the bottom of the painting an orangy or yellow cast. Using black cloth to cover the floor, on the other hand, may drink up some of the light available to the work, so do any such baffling before you begin to light the work, so that you can compensate for its effects on the evenness of the light.

If you go through all the trouble described above, the light falling across your artwork should be quite even. If your work is on the small side, and your lights at a fair distance from it—you don't want them much closer than five feet anyway—the light probably won't even need further adjustment. But if your work is at least a couple of feet square, you must fine tune the lighting, using your camera's built-in meter and the gray card described in chapter 2.

## METERING FOR EVENNESS

Be sure your camera is set to the proper ISO, or film speed. If you are following the recommendations for slide film made earlier, this will be 40, 50, 64, or possibly 160, depending on the brand and type of film. (If you're shooting black and white or color print film, the ISO will probably be 125 or 100, although these speeds may be altered slightly to achieve better negative quality, as explained in the section on shooting print films, page 102.)

With the lights on the work, and all other lights off or baffled out, place the gray card, gray side out,

Metering with a gray card.

against the middle of the work. If you have three hands, hold the card; if not, try to secure it in some way. If you can recruit someone to help you, be sure he or she doesn't cast a shadow on the setup. Make sure the card lies in the same plane as the work; holding it at an angle can throw off your readings, especially if it picks up glare from your lights.

Carefully unscrew your camera from the tripod, so as not to disturb the tripod's position. (Because you have to remove the camera to take the readings, then replace it when you're done, you may want to put off fine tuning the squareness of the artwork until after you've metered the light for evenness.) Fill the camera viewfinder with the card, but don't get so close that you cast a shadow on it yourself. There's no need to focus the camera on the card; in fact, it's best to

have the focus set to where it will be when you take the picture.

The combination of shutter speed and aperture that you use as a standard for evening the lights needn't be the same as the combination you use in actually exposing the film. In this operation, you're simply using the camera's light meter as a measuring tool in adjusting the lights. But if it makes it less confusing, refer back to chapter 2, page 32, to read about the recommendations for this combination, and set your aperture and/or shutter speed accordingly.

## METERING WITH A MANUAL CAMERA
If your camera is manual, or you're using it in a manual mode, set the lens aperture to the f-stop that seems most appropriate for your particular artwork. Then adjust the shutter speed until the needle or needles line up, the green diode

glows, or the plus and minus signs come on together—in other words, until the camera indicates correct exposure. If an in-between shutter speed seems to be required, set the longer speed and then stop the lens aperture down to obtain the proper signals. Be sure the gray card completely fills the viewfinder as you make these adjustments.

The object at this point is to take individual readings off various parts of the work, and compare them to this initial reading. If you're shooting a medium-sized work—say, in the two- or three-foot square range—take readings at the four corners of the work as well as the center. If your work is larger, you should probably take readings in the middle of the right and left sides and in the middle of the top and bottom. If in doubt, it's better to take more readings rather than fewer.

**Large Work.** Let's say your work is large. Take your gray card and place it against the work in the middle of the left side. Fill the camera viewfinder with it again, and check your match-needle, diode, or plus and minus signs. If they indicate overexposure—the needle moving up into the plus range, the diode in the "over" range glowing, or the plus symbol coming on—your light is brighter on that side than in the middle, and needs to be reduced there. To do this, first make sure the light is pointed toward the opposite edge of the work. If it is, or if you adjust it and the meter still indicates overexposure, move the light further away from the work until a "correct exposure" signal is obtained. Then double-check the center reading to see if it has fallen into the "underexposure" range. If so, you may need to move the light out slightly so that it strikes the work more directly, in order to get more light into the middle of the work. (Be watchful for glare if you do this.) As a last resort, try aiming the light beyond the far edge of the work, to take advantage of its natural fall-off in intensity.

Continue to take readings across the surface of the work, comparing them to the central reading.

1. If the readings you get at the corners or center top and bottom are off, you may need to point the lights up or down to direct more or less light at those portions of the work.
2. If the reading at the upper-right corner of the work indicates underexposure (for example), point the light on the right side up a bit, or even raise its level slightly.
3. If the top or bottom edge of the work reads underexposure all the way across, you may need

to raise or lower (respectively) both lights.

Any of these changes may also affect the light level and hence the gray card reading you get in the center of the work, so keep taking new readings there, resetting your aperture if need be. (It's easier and more precise to use the lens aperture ring rather than the shutter speed dial to fine tune the light, but be sure you use a suitably small f-stop when it comes time to make your exposures.)

Your objective is to get the gray card readings off all parts of the work as close as possible. Move the lights closer to add light when underexposure is indicated; move them farther away to subtract light when overexposure is indicated. Re-aim the lights or adjust their height when the readings at the top or bottom of the work disagree with the central reading. If all the fiddling in the world doesn't seem to produce even light, the lights may be too close, so back them both off and start again.

If you're using two lights on either side, you may have to adjust them individually, increasing their separation if the light in the horizontal center of the work is too bright, or adjusting their angles. When you're through adjusting them, even their angles may not match, particularly if the work is leaning rather than vertical.

## METERING WITH AN AUTOMATIC CAMERA

If your camera is an automatic with no manual option, you'll have to interpret the settings it selects and displays in the viewfinder. Shutter-priority automatics are the easiest to interpret. Once you've set the shutter speed, the camera will indicate an aperture when you present the gray card to it.

Say the camera indicates an aperture of f11 when you take your

first reading in the center of the work. If, when you take a reading on the side or in a corner, it indicates a setting between f11 and f16, a smaller aperture, this means that there's more light there than in the center (which is why the camera has decided that a smaller aperture is needed for proper film exposure), and that you need to reduce the light falling on that part of the artwork to make it match the central reading. As with a manual camera, you should re-aim and/or move the lights away or out until the two readings agree.

If a reading indicates a larger aperture than f11—f8, for example—this tells you that less light is falling on that portion of the work (something the camera is trying to compensate for by selecting a wider aperture), and that you need to boost it. To put it simply, *a smaller aperture than your central reading is an indication of too much light, a larger aperture an indication of less light or too little light.*

**Aperture-Priority Metering.** An aperture-priority automatic is usually harder to use in metering light in this way, because even cameras that offer stepless shutter speeds—that is, infinitely variable in-between speeds, in addition to the usual $1/125$, $1/60$, etc.—don't indicate these exact speeds in the viewfinder display. Rather, the display jumps back and forth between the official, geometric speeds, making the measurement of light levels across the surface of your work a much more approximate business. But the same technique can be applied; preset your aperture to f8 or f11, for example, look to see what shutter speed the central gray card reading indicates, then try to match that shutter speed at the other points at which you take your readings. If a slower shutter speed is indicated—$1/4$ in-

# THE COPY STAND

If your work is relatively small, and you expect to be making slides of it regularly, you may want to think about purchasing a *copy stand.* A copy stand is a stable platform with a vertical rail attached at the back; you mount your camera, lens down, on the end of a horizontal bar that's connected to the rail. The bar can be moved up or down the rail to adjust for different-sized artwork, which you place on the copy stand's *baseboard.* (Most copy stands won't accommodate work much larger than about 18" × 24" if you're using a 50mm lens.) The copy stand simplifies the squaring-up procedure greatly, because if it is well made, the camera and artwork will always be parallel to each other in the front-to-back plane. Use a bubble level to make sure they are parallel in the side-to-side plane.

- *Leveling the Camera.* Place the level on the baseboard of the copy stand, so that it runs from side to side. Note the position of the bubble. Then place the level on the back of the camera, making sure no bumps or protrusions prevent it from being parallel to the film plane. (If this isn't possible, then hold the level against the front rim of the lens instead.) Loosen the camera-mounting screw a little, and twist the camera on it until the bubble's position matches its location when on the baseboard. Make sure you don't cause the camera to shift as you tighten the screw.

    Once you've leveled the camera this way, all you need to do is adjust its height and focus. Move the artwork itself to center it in the viewfinder. Masking tape can be used to make register marks on the baseboard of the copy stand if you're shooting a number of life-sized works. If for some reason (more than likely, poor construction) the baseboard and camera aren't parallel in the front-to-back axis, you can always shim up the artwork at bottom or top to match the camera's orientation.

- *Lighting.* Lighting artwork on a copy stand is much the same as lighting vertical flat artwork, except that the lights will be pointed down at the baseboard from either side. Some fancier copy stands may even have lights attached to stalks that extend from the sides of the baseboard, but these tend to put the lights rather close to the work, and limit the size of work you can photograph to the width of the baseboard itself. All the information in this chapter about lighting angles, distances, making the light even, and exposing film is applicable to shooting work on a copy stand. If your work is quite small, the information in chapter 7 is also applicable.

stead of ⅛ second—it means that less light is present, so you must increase it. If a faster shutter speed is indicated—1/15 instead of ⅛ second—it means that more light is present, and you should decrease its level.

Whenever possible, use manual exposure control to meter your lights, both for evenness and to determine the correct exposure for your film. Never use your camera in a "program" mode; in addition to the exposure errors such a system is likely to make, it affords little control over the delicate relationship between aperture and shutter speed.

**Exposing the Film.** Review the section at the end of chapter two if you're uncertain about the details of exposing film. This section also explains how to override automatic cameras to obtain correct exposure, and how to bracket your exposures so that you have several slides of varying lightness or darkness to choose from.

You should, of course, use your gray card reading as a starting point. Make sure you hold the card flat against the center of the artwork to take the final reading. Make as many exposures on each bracket as you will need final slides, and be sure to let the camera "settle" between exposures.

Finally, remember that you can always reshoot, for minimal cost, if your first results are unsatisfactory. Before doing so, however, refer to chapter 6, "Evaluating Your Results," for help in diagnosing the problem.

## VARIATIONS ON TWO-DIMENSIONAL WORK

Although you should know enough by now to photograph most two-dimensional work, the muse—or more ordinary forces—may create

a need for the special techniques presented here. These techniques are essential if your work is either reflective or translucent, or if you must photograph it under glass.

## WORK UNDER GLASS

On occasion, you may have to shoot a print or a work on paper in a glassed frame. Any reflections on the glass will be far more noticeable in the slide or print than on a gallery wall, where a viewer can pay selective attention to the artwork underneath the reflections. While a very light piece may play down reflections on the glass, dark artwork is a particular problem because it turns the glass into a virtual mirror, reflecting you, your tripod, and anything else in the room.

One way to minimize this effect is to keep any direct light from falling on you and your tripod. (Some spill light is inevitable.) You can do this by setting up dark cards or curtains between you and the lights, or using a long lens so that your camera position will be well behind the plane of the lights. Use of the second technique may require baffling between your lights and you anyway, because of the increased risk of light entering the camera lens and causing flare.

## THE BAFFLING SOLUTION

The only really safe way of eliminating reflections on a glassed artwork is to baffle the tripod, the camera, and anything else that falls within the angle of reflection of the work, including yourself. Do this with a large piece or pieces of black poster board or matboard, or black cloth hung from the ceiling.

If you use a black card, you'll have to cut a hole in the middle of it to poke the lens through. Use the rim of the lens as a template for the hole by placing it against the middle of the board and drawing around it. Don't make the hole any larger than it needs to be, or else some of

the metal parts of the camera may show through and be reflected by the glass on the artwork. If the hole is cut fairly precisely, so that it fits the lens snugly, and the board is reasonably stiff, the lens will actually support it, sparing you the need to hold it or otherwise support it with tape or rods. You can even attach it to the lens with tape (black photographic tape if on the front), but be sure to focus the lens before doing so, and be careful not to move the focusing ring when you do attach it. If you use black cloth, you can cut a slit in it to slip the lens through. Because of its lack of rigidity, if you use cloth as a baffling material it will have to be suspended from above, either from the ceiling or a rod or bar of some sort above the camera. A wooden dowel running between two ladders, one on either side of the camera, is one possibility. You may have to support a large or flimsy piece of cardboard or posterboard in a similar way.

**More Is Less.** The size of the card or piece of cloth you will need depends on the size of the artwork. The larger the area of a glassed work, the more of its surroundings it will reflect, and the larger the card or cloth has to be. It almost always needs to be larger than you think it does, so be generous with whatever material you are using. The best way to determine the size you need is to look through the camera, or stand directly behind it with your eyes just above it, and extend your arms to either side, waving your hands. (Use a stick if your arms aren't long enough.) Observe their reflection, and note where it passes out of the image area of the work. If all but your hand is reflected in the glass, the card has to be at least as wide as your armspan, wrist to wrist. Very large works may require cards or

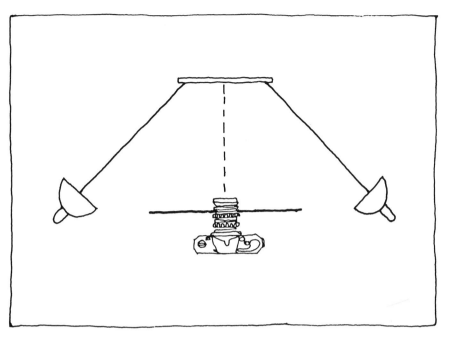

## WORK UNDER GLASS

A large black card with a hole cut to size in the middle to poke the lens through will eliminate reflections on a glassed work. To create reflections off shiny material in an artwork, substitute a white card.

cloth larger than what's available, so you may have to set up additional cards or curtains to either side of your main baffle.

When you've set up the baffling cards, look through the viewfinder to see if you've managed to block out the entire reflection. Even a small fragment of the original reflection—a tripod leg, a piece of masking tape—can be very distracting in the wrong place. Cover any such offending areas with black tape, cloth, or paper. In some circumstances, your baffling materials may absorb a small amount of the light illuminating the work, so be sure to bracket your exposures well on the "over" side.

As you shoot your pictures, be sure the reflection-baffling rig doesn't jar the camera during the exposure, a particular risk if you must hold the baffle. It's better to secure the baffle to eliminate this as a possible cause of lack of sharpness in your photographs.

**Filters Aren't the Answer.** Artists having a little familiarity with photographic technique may be under the impression that a polarizing filter can be used to eliminate reflections on glass. This filter, described more fully in chapter 9, will eliminate or minimize reflections when they are at a fairly steep angle to the camera and reflective surface, but won't eliminate the sort of direct reflection that occurs when you photograph a glassed artwork.

## REFLECTIVE MATERIALS IN FLAT ARTWORK

If your artwork contains reflective materials such as foil, gold leaf, pieces of mirror or metal, glitter or sequins, you may find that lighting it from the sides doesn't produce the kind of shininess you'd like. Oddly enough, the solution to this problem is quite similar to that for eliminating reflections in glass. Simply substitute a white card or sheet for the black one, cutting a hole in it for the lens, as described previously. The white surface (which is, in effect, bounce-lighted

by the light reflected off the work itself) will give the shiny materials something to reflect.

## LARGE WORK

If your work is large, you may be so far away from it that a white card or sheet used in this way doesn't reflect enough light back to the piece. If this is the case, you may need to throw some light back into it using a third or fourth bulb (fifth or sixth, if you're lighting the work with two lamps on either side). A regular lightbulb is OK to use for this purpose, as long as it doesn't contribute a significant part of the light falling on the surface of the work. Just be very sure that none of the light enters the camera lens, and that it doesn't create glare on the surface of the work.

Using bounce light such as this is a relatively safe way of creating reflections in the work, but sometimes even turning on an ordinary household bulb at your camera position will produce enough reflection on the shiny portions of the work. A 100-watt bulb is usually

# VIDEO

A still photograph can only represent a moment in a videotape, but it may be useful to support other materials, and to serve as a "reminder" to anyone considering your work. It also may be necessary to provide slides of a videotape for use in a catalogue.

As simple as it may seem, you must keep a number of things in mind when photographing a television screen or video monitor, most of them relating to its characteristics as a light source for its own imagery. First of all, you should use daylight, not tungsten film; it will produce more accurate color, although your result may still appear somewhat blue-green, a color combination called cyan in photography. Use of a relatively strong (CC 30 or 40) red filter over the camera lens will eliminate this cast, but knowledgeable videographers may be able to adjust the monitor's color balance to accomplish this. Black and white televisions tend to photograph very blue/cyan, and may require heavy yellow filtration to record as a neutral gray on film.

Also, eliminate any strong ambient light sources, to prevent reflections on the surface of the screen. (For the same reason, don't ever use flash to photograph a TV screen.) And if the image you've chosen to photograph has bright highlights and deep low values, it may reproduce better if you reduce the monitor's contrast. Video images appear higher in contrast in a photograph than when actually viewed. Because of this, you should also adjust the brightness control so that detail is visible in both light and dark areas.

You will need a tripod to photograph off a TV monitor, both to maintain squareness and to permit the use of slower shutter speeds. Because the shape of the screen is a rectangle with bowed sides, you can "square" it up reasonably well with the method described on page 42. Essentially, you want the camera to be lined up with the center of the screen, to avoid distortion of its shape. Keep the room lights on when you set up your camera so that you can use the frame of the TV itself as a reference. Make the screen fill the viewfinder, but leave enough room around it so that its curved sides won't be cropped by the slide mount. Particularly when a video image is reduced to 35mm size, the shape of the screen is important in indicating that the image is from a videotape. Smaller TV/monitor screens may require the use of close-up attachments if the closest focusing distance of your lens won't let you fill the viewfinder with the screen. Don't get too far away from the monitor; not only will the slide be less dramatic, but the camera's meter may be thrown off by the large dark area surrounding the screen.

The best practice is to take your meter reading directly off the screen to determine your starting exposure. (If you're using a color-correcting filter in front of the lens, the camera's meter should put you in the ballpark, provided the video image has a variety of colors.) When you take the reading, try to crop out as much of the surrounding dark area as possible, and include as much of the screen as you can. An automatic camera will "correct" its reading when you frame up the monitor with the dark areas surrounding it, so you will have to override it with the exposure compensation control or ISO dial, or lock the previous settings in if the camera has a provision for doing so. To make the camera accept the previous settings with the exposure compensation control or ISO dial, use the technique described in chapters 2 and 3 for making an automatic camera's averaged reading match the settings indicated by the gray card reading.

Use of shutter speeds much faster than 1/8 second can result in the appearance of dark bands in a photograph of a videotape image, if the tape is running. Such slow speeds may be insufficient, however, to freeze movement in the tape, either in the subject or from one shot to the next. Freeze-framing can solve this problem, but it may cause other kinds of distortion. Experiment to determine how fast a shutter speed you can use while still maintaining acceptable image quality. If there's no time for this, make a number of exposures at different shutter speeds from 1/8 to 1/30 second, bracketing your exposures with lens aperture changes at each speed. Even if you've established a good shutter speed, because of the variable nature of video imagery, it's important to bracket your exposures heavily.

too dim to cause glare problems.

## STAINED GLASS

Stained glass is perhaps the trickiest kind of two-dimensional artwork to photograph, because it must be *transilluminated*—lighted from behind. Never shine a light directly through a stained glass window to photograph it. Even if the window is opaque enough to diffuse the light, doing so will not produce an even result.

To shoot stained glass that's not installed, you will need to find a way to support it that allows for a clear, unobstructed area behind the work. If the piece is mounted in a wooden frame, you may be able to stand it on the far edge of a table. Alternatively, you can support it with guy wires to the ceiling or walls, or a sturdy length of dowel, lattice, or strapping across the top. (This support system can be masked out in the finished slide.) You must leave enough room around the work not only to shoot it from the front, but to light it evenly from the back, as described below.

## BACKLIGHTING WITH A DIFFUSION SCRIM

The easiest way to light stained glass is by placing a sheet of diffusion material behind it, then illuminating the material from the back. White plastic bags, translucent shower curtains, and the like can be used, provided they have no visible texture or color. White bed sheets aren't as good because they transmit light less readily and may show their texture through transparent glass if close enough to the back of the piece. They will also require much longer exposures. Commercial diffusion films that are ideally suited to this purpose are sold by professional photography stores in rolls or by the running foot. Tracing vellum can even be

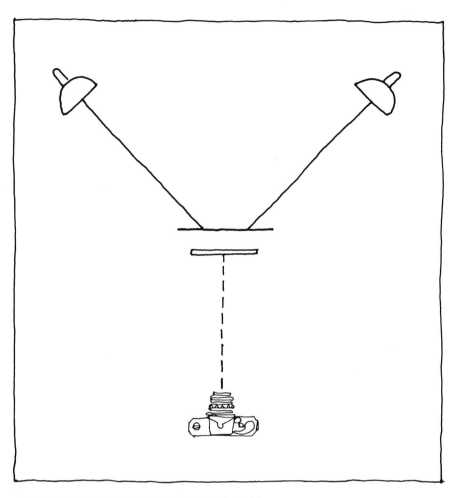

## BASIC LIGHTING FOR STAINED GLASS

A sheet of diffusion material is placed behind the work, then backlighted evenly from the sides. Baffling cards, not indicated here, should be carefully placed so that no direct light enters the lens.

used if you are careful not to get the lights too close to it. Be sure any material you purchase or use is wide enough to fill the entire glass area from your camera position. Scope out the piece with your camera, if you haven't already set it up, to determine this.

Use as many bulbs as necessary to produce even light across the diffusion surface, remembering that the loss of brightness and requirements of evenness will probably demand at least two bulbs. You can, however, light the diffusion surface at a somewhat more direct angle than you would a painting, as shown in the diagram on page 55. Use your camera's meter to make the light across the diffusion surface even, adjusting the lights in the same ways described earlier in this chapter. You can take your meter readings directly off the white surface of the diffusion material, although the indicated combination of aperture and shutter speed will have no direct bearing on your final exposure. You can meter off the front surface of the material or the back, but be sure no light from the bulbs enters the lens directly as you take your readings.

## BOUNCE LIGHT

An alternative method to the backlighted scrim is to bounce light off white paper, a white sheet, or a white card behind the piece. One drawback to this is that the bounce surface must be placed further from the work than a backlighted diffusion surface, to make room for the lights and allow even illumination of the surface. This in turn requires the use of a larger surface area of material. It also tends to make less efficient use of the bulbs' output than the diffusion technique, depending on the thickness of the diffusion material.

In shooting stained glass, it's also not a bad idea to throw some light on the front surface of the glass, just as if you were lighting a regular flat artwork. This will give a sense of substance and detail to the leading, and is absolutely necessary if your piece contains opaque glass, which often reflects as much light off its front surface as it transmits, depending on lighting conditions. The light on the front surface of the glass, however, should be two or three stops dimmer than that passing through it, depending on the degree of transparency in the glass itself. This can

be accomplished by placing the lights farther away from the front surface, using lamps of lower wattage, or bouncing or diffusing the lights to reduce their intensity. Unless your frontlighting is considerably brighter than this (which may be necessary for very dense glass), it shouldn't affect the exposure, which is based on the backlighting, as we'll see.

## EXPOSING FOR STAINED GLASS

Determining the correct exposure for stained glass is almost as tricky as the setup required to shoot it, because it comes in such a variety of translucencies and opacities. If by chance your piece transmits, on average, the same amount of light that a light meter is calibrated for—the 18 percent reflection of the gray card—you can probably get a reliable exposure simply by using the settings that an automatic camera chooses or that a manual camera recommends when you fill the viewfinder with the artwork.

It's likely, though, that your piece transmits more or less light than this, so it's better to use the known brightness of the backlighted or bounce-lighted surface that is providing the light as a way of determining the correct exposure. This is as simple as taking a reading off the surface itself (again, making sure that no direct light strays into the lens if the surface is backlighted), then increasing your exposure by four stops. This adjustment allows you to obtain an exposure equivalent to that which would be indicated by the reading off a front-lighted gray card (which is considerably less bright) in a conventional setup.

In other words, if your meter reading off the illuminated surface (the side facing the work) is $^1/_{60}$ second at f11, use $^1/_4$ second at f11 as your starting exposure. If it is $^1/_8$

second at f22 (a function of your automatic camera's priority or where you happen to have your manual camera's controls set), use $^1/_8$ second at f5.6 as your starting exposure. As always, you can combine aperture and shutter speed changes to achieve the increase in exposure, too. If your indicated reading is $^1/_{30}$ second at f11, and you're reluctant to reduce your shutter speed to $^1/_4$ second, you can reduce it to $^1/_8$ second to gain three stops of exposure, then open the aperture a stop to f5.6 for the fourth.

Whatever starting exposure you use to photograph stained glass, it is even more important to bracket your exposures broadly than with other kinds of work. Bracket them at least a stop in either direction, remembering not to risk overly wide apertures, and to keep the shutter speed within the limits required by the film. If respecting these constraints becomes a problem, either boost the light levels or use a higher-speed film.

**Glass Values.** Stained glass works which contain areas of extremely different translucence may produce a slide with far too much contrast, in which either the very transparent parts are washed out or the more opaque ones are too dark. The only practical solution to this problem is to mask the very clear parts of the piece with tracing vellum or translucent diffusion film. The film must be cut to the exact shape of the areas to be masked, and carefully and invisibly applied to the back of the work. (You can use small, strategically placed pieces of transparent tape.) This may, however, make an absolutely clear piece of glass appear frosted. You can use your meter to measure the change in transmission that masking causes, but the only sure way of testing the balance between light and dark glass is to shoot a test. If the light areas still seem washed out, use another (or a thicker) layer of diffusion film.

A quick, if less certain, way of shooting stained glass is to prop it up in a window during the day. Be sure the window has no direct sunlight coming through it. Place a smooth sheet of tracing vellum or diffusing film behind the artwork to further diffuse the light and eliminate the background. Make sure none of the frame or lattice of the window intrudes into the glass of the piece. Use daylight film with a warming filter (81A). You can take meter readings off the diffusion sheet and adjust your exposure as explained, or take an averaged reading off the glass and bracket your exposures heavily.

## INSTALLED STAINED GLASS

You have fewer options, and less control, if you're shooting stained glass that's installed. An installed work is probably backlighted with daylight, in which case you must shoot daylight-balanced film. A modest amount of tungsten light falling on the inside of the window shouldn't create a serious color temperature problem; in fact, you may want to boost the level of front light, to give detail to the leading and surfaces of the glass. (Just be sure it's from enough of an angle to prevent glare.)

Because you can't meter the light source as described above, take your reading off the window itself, making sure to crop out any dark surrounding areas which might cause overexposure. If your camera is automatic, lock in those settings, or adjust the exposure compensation control or ISO dial when you recompose the piece so that the settings match those indicated by the reading off the window. Be sure to bracket your exposures heavily in both directions.

## SUMMARY/ **TWO-DIMENSIONAL WORK**

- Position your artwork securely in a place with good clearance to the front and sides of the work.
- Set the tripod up at a distance from which the artwork roughly fills the camera's viewfinder. Raise the camera to a height that falls along an imaginary line from the middle of the work.
- Attach the camera securely to the tripod's mounting platform, and adjust its angle to match that of the work.
- Fine tune the camera's distance from the work, and square the artwork up by manipulating the controls of the tripod, moving it if necessary. Use the sides of the viewfinder frame as a reference for squareness.
- Position your lights to either side of the camera. Don't make their angle on the work any steeper that 45 degrees; if you see glare when you look through the viewfinder, make the angle more oblique (i.e., move the lights closer to the plane of the work, so that they strike it at more of an angle). If you're using a single light on either side, raise them to a height corresponding to the middle of the work.
- Take meter readings off the gray card at the center, corner, and sides of the work to measure the evenness of the light. By adjusting the lamps' angle, height and/or distance from the work, increase the light level in areas that are less bright than the center, and decrease the light level in areas that are brighter. The end result should be that the readings are consistent across the entire surface of the work.
- Choose your final combination of aperture and shutter speed, checking to make sure the gray card reading indicates that this combination will produce proper exposure at the ISO you have set.
- If your camera is automatic, make the necessary adjustments to the exposure compensation control or ISO dial to obtain this combination.
- Focus the lens carefully and take your pictures, making sure to bracket the exposure fully.
- To photograph work under glass, baffle the camera and anything else the glass reflects with black paper, board, or cloth.
- To photograph work containing shiny materials, place white paper, cards, or cloth around the camera to provide something bright for the materials to reflect.
- To photograph stained glass, place a sheet of translucent film or vellum behind the work, then light it evenly from the back. Bracket your exposures heavily.

# FOUR THREE-DIMENSIONAL WORK

In technique, what distinguishes the photography of three-dimensional work from that of flat work is the nature of the light itself. While the even, direct light appropriate for two-dimensional artwork simply insures that the film will record the work's tones and colors in their true relationships, the kind of light needed in photographing sculptural work has a modeling function: it describes contours, textures, and shapes. For this reason, it generally must be softer and more unidirectional than the light used for flat work. Use of direct light from more than one source can create confusing shadows on a three-dimensional work, and multiple shadows across the background against which it's photographed.

The other difference in photographing three-dimensional work is that, with the exception of times you want to show a work *in situ,* you will probably want to shoot it on a background of plain, uninterrupted paper, known in the trade as a "seamless." While cloth can be used in some circumstances, paper is better because its stiffness makes it easier to control.

## 3-D EQUIPMENT

The information you've gotten thus far on films, photolamps, and general technique applies to sculptural as well as flat work. But the differences may warrant the purchase of another few items of photographic "software." One of these is a photographic *umbrella,* a less-than-waterproof version of the real thing. Its white or silver lining acts as a reflector, bouncing the light from your bulbs back at a sculptural work in a much softer and more flattering way. White boards, sheets, or even strategically located white walls and ceilings may be used in a similar fashion, but they reflect light in a less efficient and even more diffuse way than does the parabolic shape of an umbrella. Some photographic umbrellas are made of translucent material so that they may be used as diffusers, too.

Photographic umbrellas can be purchased in a good professional photography store. They cost anywhere from twenty to forty-five dollars, depending on their size and style, and must be secured in some way at the appropriate position. Fixtures for this purpose, designed to mount on lightstands, are also available, although clamps and duct tape will also do the job. Umbrellas with a silver lining are even more reflective than those with white linings, but the light from them will have a more focused quality, producing a slightly more contrasty image.

## A SUITABLE BACKGROUND

Another expense in shooting sculptural work is for the background material. Although this can be as little as the cost of a large sheet of drawing paper, something you may even have on hand, it might be as much as the price of a roll of seamless background paper, or a piece of Formica or Plexiglas.

Seamless background paper is available in various colors from most professional photography stores. You may have to special-order it, particularly if you want an offbeat color, so plan ahead. It comes in rolls of four-, nine-, and twelve-foot widths, each twelve yards long. The four-foot roll should cost you something over fifteen dollars, the nine-foot twenty-five plus. Store the unused portions of the roll tightly coiled and

**PHOTOGRAPHIC UMBRELLA**

The white or silver lining of the umbrella acts as a reflector to bounce the light from the bulbs back at a sculpture in a soft and flattering way.

Ralph Helmick

## EFFECT OF BACKGROUND ON SCULPTURAL WORK

The color or tone of your seamless background paper can have a strong effect on the appearance of the artwork in the photograph. In the photograph at top left, a white seamless makes the background virtually disappear, emphasizing the shape of the work. However, because the white ground bounces light into the shadows of the piece, it appears to be somewhat flatly lighted. The artwork was lighted in exactly the same way for the photograph at bottom left, but placed on a medium gray seamless instead. This change makes the light seem much more dramatic. Notice that the highlights on the fingers and palm stand out more strongly, but that the shadows tend to merge with the background tone, emphasizing the work's shape less effectively than the treatment at left. If you're shooting your work against a white ground, you may choose to diffuse your light source less heavily, to create more contrast between highlights and shadows. In some cases, direct light may even be appropriate, although you might have to create additional fill light with reflectors.

upright. When the portion you've been using becomes dirty, scuffed, or torn, you can roll out another length.

For smaller objects, other kinds of paper and flexible boards can be used, and may even be preferable if they have a less visible texture than seamless background paper. (The smaller the object, the closer you must place the camera to it, and the more visible the texture of the background paper will be.) Good-quality poster board and matboard are useful, although if you plan to shoot a free-standing object on them, be sure they are flexible enough to be bent into a smooth 90-degree curve. (This is necessary to produce a continuous background.) If you want to photograph your piece against a white background, bristol board is an excellent choice, although many drawing papers will suffice.

**Color and Contrast.** Seamless background papers are manufactured in several dozen colors, as are poster boards and matboards. Ask your professional photo dealer to show you a sample book. But be forewarned: like paint swatches, a small sample can be misleading; be conservative, particularly if you are special-ordering a roll sight unseen. In most instances, a white or light-to-medium gray will do the most justice to your artwork, and be the least distracting. There are exceptions—gold jewelry looks beautiful on a royal blue velvet, for example. But in general, avoid bright colors; depending on your lighting arrangement, they may even affect the artwork's color. Your objective should be to show the work as clearly and simply as possible. Curators will thank you.

Think about the *contrast* between background and artwork, as well as the color. (If you're using black and white film, this should be the main consideration.) A light object—of silver, marble, clear plastic—will "read" better on a background deeper in tone, such as a medium gray. A black background can be very dramatic, but use it with caution. A darker object—of oxidized metal, clay, or some kinds of wood—will probably look better on a white or medium gray. If photographing a very dark object, you may choose to shoot against a medium gray rather than white, because the additional exposure a dark object sometimes needs may cause the background to be rendered lighter than it appears, and a light gray ground will retain some tone in such a case, whereas a white ground might go blank.

## OTHER BACKGROUND MATERIALS

There are several alternatives to paper backgrounds. Cloth is a possibility, but because it is hard to shape into a smooth curve without a support, it works best when it can be hung behind the artwork, rather than running underneath it. (Artworks that can be suspended or cropped at their pedestals are well suited to this treatment.) As a background, black cloth will appear blacker than black paper, but even it will usually have a texture visible in the slide. The smaller the artwork, the more pronounced any texture will be. Black velvet, velour, or velveteen don't have a visible warp and woof, and similar napped materials absorb more light than regular woven cloth, which makes them look blacker in a photograph. Any cloth background must be supported underneath by a rigid, curved surface if the object is to sit on it.

**Canvas.** There are also commercial background materials made of heavy canvas, hand-painted with abstract muted brushed patterns. These can be bought from mail-order sources like the ones listed in the "Useful Accessories" appendix, although a professional dealer may be able to special-order them for you. They aren't cheap, and you can probably duplicate them yourself. There's no harm in experimenting; paint-splattered dropcloths, old, low-pile monochrome rugs, and the like, may produce useful effects in some circumstances. A very smooth-surfaced, minimal piece of sculpture, for example, might benefit from the contrast of a rough, stippled background. But be conservative!

**Formica.** Formica—available from building supply outfits, good lumber yards, and even well-supplied hardware stores—makes an excellent background surface, as strange as it may sound. It's flexible enough to bend into a nice, smooth curve, although because it wants to spring back flat, you will have to attach it securely to the table and wall you're working with. Because it's quite scratch-resistant, Formica will last indefinitely, unlike seamless paper. Its durability offsets its higher price—about a dollar and a half a square foot. Buy it in a matte finish to minimize reflections. A medium gray is a good all-purpose choice.

**Plexiglas.** Even Plexiglas has its applications, although because it's shiny you must be careful in positioning your lights. You usually have to buy it at a plastics specialty shop. Jewelry, glossy ceramic work, or any piece with a high-tech appearance looks particularly snappy against black Plexiglas. And one way to prevent a shiny object—whether glazed or metallic—from reflecting the color of the ground it's sitting on is to float it on a clear Plexiglas surface, with the colored background behind or several feet beneath it. Although this technique is somewhat advanced,

## SIDE VIEW, BASIC THREE-DIMENSIONAL SETUP

Don't place the artwork too close to the curve of the seamless, or else the shadow it casts may curve up the background. Keep in mind that the higher the light source, the shorter the shadow will be.

it will be described briefly later in this chapter. Translucent (milky) Plexiglas can be used when you want to eliminate shadows on the background, or make it disappear into a blank white. You do this by illuminating the background from behind, a technique which will also be described later.

Plexiglas comes in different weights. Unless you are shooting down on an object, and only need a flat, rigid background, be sure that you buy a sheet that's thin enough to bend into the smooth curve that free-standing artworks will require. The larger your artwork, the thicker it can be, because the curve in a larger sheet of Plexiglas will be more gradual. An eighth of an inch is a good thickness for medium-sized works.

### FILL THE SPACE

Whether you use Formica, Plexiglas, cloth, or paper, be sure your material is both wide and long enough to fill the entire viewfinder when your camera is at the proper distance from the artwork. Keep in mind that as the background material recedes from the artwork and the camera, its lateral coverage is reduced, and its edges may appear in the upper corners of the viewfinder. And if you must get closer to the work, whether for a detail or to make it fill the frame with a wider-than-normal-angle lens, the change in perspective will reduce the coverage of the background material. Also, because of the long, gradual curve required in a seamless background, you will need a surprisingly *long* piece. You won't know the exact needs of your artwork until you've set it up, so when in doubt, overestimate.

### THE SETUP

If your artwork is small, it may be

easier to photograph it on a sturdy table. If it's large, use the floor, but in either case, work against a wall that's free of windows, woodwork, or hanging objects.

Unless you intend to "shoot down" against a flat background—a treatment that works well for jewelry or the interior of bowls—you will have to attach the leading edge of your background paper or board to the wall, well above the highest point of your artwork. Use strong tape, pushpins, or both. Then roll the paper out, allowing it to form a smooth curve on its way down to the table or floor. Roll it out generously on the surface your artwork will rest on; you don't want the artwork too close to the curve, or else any shadow it casts will be distorted. And make sure the curve isn't too abrupt.

If you're using seamless background paper, handle it carefully to avoid crimping or tearing, and cut the proper length of paper from the roll with a mat knife or scissors. Store the remainder of the roll tightly coiled and upright, to prevent the formation of bumps and dimples in its surface. Secure the front edge of your background material to your working surface.

If you're handy and ambitious, you may be able to improvise a free-standing support for the roll of seamless. In professional studios, the entire roll of seamless is hung on a metal rod which is supported by two vertical spring-compressed posts running between ceiling and floor. Paper is then rolled out as needed.

## POSITIONING THE ARTWORK

If you're photographing your work against a flat background, its proper placement should be self-evident. If you're using a curved seamless ground, be sure the work is far enough forward on it so that any shadow it may cast doesn't fol-

low the curve of the ground. On the other hand, if the vertical portion of the seamless is too far away from the work, it may end up much darker in your photograph. This effect can be quite dramatic in shooting light artwork, but may also result in a strong bluish cast if you're using a white background. None of this will be fully apparent until you establish your lighting arrangement.

If the artwork is heavy or has sharp edges, be careful not to tear or scratch the background when you position it. If you're shooting a large object and must walk on the background paper to position it, put clean sheets of paper down to protect it from footprints. In any case, be sure the side of the artwork that you want to photograph is facing directly toward your camera position. Once you establish the proper camera-to-artwork distance, look through your camera from that point to make sure the seamless fills the frame.

## SETTING UP THE CAMERA

It's best to set up the camera and tripod before positioning the light or lights, because their placement will probably affect your lighting arrangement. You can throw some casual light on the artwork to make framing and focusing easier, though.

Make the artwork fill the frame, whether horizontal or vertical, but don't cramp it. If it doesn't conform to the image area of your 35mm camera, remember that a finished slide can be masked to eliminate empty areas, and a print cropped. (This will be covered in chapter 7.) Consider the height of the camera carefully. A slightly elevated position will show the top of a piece as well as its sides, but may tend to make the upper portions of the piece loom, an effect that can be minimized by the use of a lens of

longer focal length, as described below. A low camera position may make the artwork seem more monumental than it is, or simply emphasize its monumentality. If this treatment appeals to you, be sure the background material extends far enough above the top of the piece to fill the viewfinder frame. By and large, it's best not to make the photograph's perspective on the piece too distracting. Let the artwork speak for itself.

## LENSES AND THREE-DIMENSIONAL WORK

In shooting three-dimensional work, many professional photographers opt to use lenses of longer focal length than the standard 50mm, usually in the moderate telephoto range, from 85- or 90mm to 135mm. This is because such a lens can have the effect of making the parts of a sculptural work appear to be in truer proportion to one another. The lens does this simply by the change in perspective (i.e., distance from the work) that its narrower angle of view requires; in other words, you must be farther away from the work to fit the whole thing into the viewfinder frame. This requirement may prevent you from using a long lens, even if you have access to one, because your space may be too small, your work too large, or both. If your artwork is small, on the other hand, the closest focusing distance of a longer lens may place you too far away from a small artwork to fill the frame with it.

Some newer zoom lenses offer a "macro" mode which will allow close focusing down to as little as half a foot. You'll find that these lenses are a viable alternative to macro lenses and close-up attachments, if the work you are photographing is small. It's especially important, though, to select smaller lens apertures if you are using a

35mm lens

50mm lens

## EFFECT OF DIFFERENT FOCAL-LENGTH LENSES ON SCULPTURAL WORK

The *focal length* of a lens (see chapter 1 for a complete definition) also has a dramatic effect on the way an artwork is represented in a photograph. The focal length of a lens determines how far from the artwork your camera must be to make the work fill the frame, and this in turn affects the perspective with which it will be represented. In the pictures above, for example, the wider-angle lenses (35mm and 50mm) require that the camera be closer to the piece to make it fill the frame, resulting in an image in which more of the base is visible, and in which the fingers seem to loom forward. By contrast, the fingers in the 105mm "telephoto" lens shot, left, seem more in proportion to the rest of the hand, but less of the top surface of the artwork's base is visible—all because the lens forces you to shoot the piece from farther away. Which treatment you prefer is really a matter of taste, and of what aspect of the work you want to emphasize. However, in the 35mm shot—included to show how a fixed-lens automatic compact camera might render the piece—the relationship between the wrist and fingers is quite distorted. It's rarely appropriate to use anything wider than a 50mm lens in photographing artwork, either two- or three-dimensional.

105mm lens

long lens or a zoom set for macro mode to shoot small work. Refer to the section on shooting small work, page 96, for further information.

**Large Works.** On the other extreme, if your work is very large relative to your working space, you may find that the standard 50- or 55mm lens doesn't have a wide enough field of view to fit the work into the frame. In such a case, you either have to relocate to a larger space, or use a slightly wide-angle lens such as a 35mm lens, which will permit you to include more of the work from the same distance. ("35mm" here refers to the lens' focal length, not the 35mm film format of the camera itself.) The price of this advantage is considerable distortion, depending on the nature of the work; the parts of it closest to the camera will seem disproportionately large.

The fixed lenses on automatic 35mm compact non-SLR cameras are moderately wide-angle, usually from 35 to 40mm in focal length, so they will distort the artwork as well. You can minimize the distortion caused by a wide-angle lens by moving farther away from the work, but this will of course reduce the size of the work on the resulting film. If you're shooting slides, this is probably unacceptable; if you're shooting film for the sole purpose of making prints, you can have a custom lab enlarge and crop the image to size, or have a commercial photo finisher make a print a size larger than you need, then trim it.

## ZOOM TO THE RESCUE
A zoom lens of moderately wide-angle to medium-telephoto range—for example, 28 to 80mm or 35 to 70mm—may bail you out in the kind of tight shooting situation that a 50mm lens is too long for. Setting it in the 40-odd mm range

will allow you to include more of the work without the distortion likely from a 35mm lens, which is the nearest wide-angle alternative in a lens of fixed focal length. Always use the lens at its longest possible setting to minimize distortion: in other words, get as far away from the artwork as possible, then adjust the zoom setting to make the artwork fill the frame. If space allows, you should certainly use such a lens at its 50mm setting, or beyond.

## LIGHTING THREE-DIMENSIONAL WORK
Because of its tremendous variety, three-dimensional work has no hard-and-fast rules for lighting. Keep in mind that the function of light is not simply to make the piece bright enough to shoot at reasonable camera settings, but to describe its contours, surfaces, and shapes. Sometimes this description is the result of shadows the artwork casts on itself, which create a sense of volume. But be sure that any shadows on the work don't obscure important features.

In shooting three-dimensional work, it's advisable to stick with a unidirectional light source. This avoids confusing multiple shadows on the work and background. With certain kinds of work or interpretations, this single source can be direct and undiffused, creating a dramatic, high-contrast effect which usually produces shadows that must be "filled in" with reflectors placed outside the camera's field of view. Most work, however, is better served by a softer kind of light. One way to soften the light is by *bouncing* it.

## BOUNCE LIGHT
Bounce lighting is most easily accomplished with a photographic umbrella, described at the begin-

ning of this chapter. You "aim" the inside of the umbrella at the work, and point your lights back into it. You can also bounce light back into the work with a large white card or board or white sheet. If it's convenient, you can even use an adjacent wall or low ceiling as a bounce surface, but be sure it's a white of relatively neutral tone. Even a warm white wall will color the work somewhat if light is bounced off it. Flat, white bounce surfaces such as these tend to be less efficient reflectors than photographic umbrellas.

Because of the loss of brightness involved in bounce lighting (often several "stops"), it's not a bad idea to use two bulbs, both pointed at the same reflector. This will reduce the need for very long shutter speeds or wide apertures that might compromise your depth of field, an important consideration in shooting three-dimensional work.

## DIFFUSED LIGHT
A somewhat more efficient alternative to bounce lighting is *diffusing* a light that's aimed directly at your artwork with a piece of translucent plastic. White garbage bags—one side only, to reduce light loss—work well, as do old shower curtains, as long as they have no visible color. (Even if they don't, they often have a slight warming effect on the color of the slide.) You can also buy a commercial photographic diffusion film, usually available by the running foot at a professional photography store. It comes in different degrees of translucency; get one that's neither so thick it really cuts down on your light levels, nor so thin that it doesn't adequately soften your light.

Whether you're bouncing your light or diffusing it, be sure your bounce surfaces or diffusers are at

## BIRD'S-EYE VIEW, BASIC THREE-DIMENSIONAL SETUP

Direct light, page 66, is rarely flattering to an artwork because it creates heavy, empty shadows. But if a white reflector card is placed off-camera next to the side of the work opposite the light source, page 67, these shadows can be filled in. Although this treatment may be useful for artworks in which you want to enhance texture, a softer light is generally more suited to sculptural work. The latter defines the contours of an artwork more effectively, and the shadows it creates are less harsh, although you may still choose to use a reflector to lighten them. You can soften the light by bouncing it into a white or silver-lined photographic umbrella, page 66, or by diffusing it with a sheet of translucent film, page 67, or even a white plastic bag.

a reasonable distance from your lamps—several feet, if possible. This is both a safety consideration—the bulbs burn hot enough to melt or set fire to materials that are too close—and a practical one. To create a broad, soft light, the bulb's beam must encompass a good portion of the bounce or diffusion surface. For this reason, you have to use a reflector or diffuser of reasonable size. A one-foot square, for example, won't do the job. The larger the work, the more surface area you'll need for equivalent softness. Because different works of art may vary in terms of the quality of light that is most becoming to them, it's difficult to give exact figures; be generous. Experiment with and observe the effect of different combinations of distance and diffusion surface area, both of which will affect the quality as well as the intensity of the light.

**Diffusion Hangups.** Supporting and securing the bounce or diffusion surface will also require a little improvisational skill, although there are the usual commercial alternatives, in this case a rod that may be attached horizontally to a light stand with a special fixture. If you're using a stiff card for bounce lighting, it can be clipped or taped onto a ladder or an exposed pipe, for example. A sheet can be suspended from the ceiling, but may need to be angled down toward the work by guying back its lower edge with tape or string. Diffusion materials can be similarly supported. Heavy wooden dowels are useful for these purposes, and can be pur-·chased at lumber yards or good hardware stores. You can even use a prefab commercial painting stretcher to keep a piece of diffusion material taut, or build one yourself, but keep it light if you intend to clip or tape it onto its supports.

A

B

C

## EFFECT OF VARIATIONS IN LIGHTING TECHNIQUE

In photograph A, the artwork was lighted from a fairly high angle in front of and to the right of it, using a single lamp diffused with a piece of translucent film. In the second photograph, B, the piece was lighted with an undiffused lamp in more or less the same position, creating much deeper shadows than the diffused light. In the third shot, C, a neutral white card was placed to the right and in front of the piece, angled so that it would bounce as much of the direct light into the shadows as possible. Using reflector cards in this way can soften the harsh effect of direct light considerably, and allows you to take advantage of its surface-defining quality without creating distractingly deep shadows on the piece. Photograph D shows the effect of a badly placed light source. Not only does the light fail to describe the contours of the piece, but it causes it to cast a distracting shadow on the background. Although you should always position your light source so that it best defines the work's contours, be conscious of where its shadow is thrown. If a strong shadow is inevitable, it can be played down by filling it in with reflectors or auxiliary lights.

## PLACING AND ADJUSTING YOUR LIGHT SOURCE

In photographing three-dimensional work, your light source should generally be positioned above and to the side of the camera, unless your camera position is quite distant, as in photographing a large piece or using a telephoto lens. In these cases, you may want to place the light and softening paraphernalia closer to the work to maximize its brightness. Be sure that it still illuminates the work and background fully, and be careful not to let it intrude into the picture area. You must also be careful not to let direct light from the bulb enter the camera's lens, carefully placing baffling cards to block it out, if need be. Aim your reflector, umbrella, or, if diffusing the light, your bulbs at the center of the work or even below, so that the lower portions receive as much light as the top.

## TOP LIGHT

Some three-dimensional artworks look better in light that comes from above. Usually such *top light* (for examples, see color section page 106) works better if it's softened by bouncing or diffusion, but with certain pieces, even the light from a single, undiffused bulb may be appropriate.

The simplest way to create soft top light is to aim the lamps—you should use at least two 500-watt bulbs, because of the reduction in light intensity caused by bouncing—at a low, neutral-white ceiling. If your ceilings aren't low enough, you can substitute a large piece of white board or a sheet, suspending it horizontally over the work. If you're going to this amount of trouble, however, you can make more efficient use of the light available from your lamps by suspending a piece of diffusion material instead, and aiming the lamps through it.

Whether you're bouncing or diffusing your lamps, keep them slightly in front of the front surface of the work. Because this technique will tend to make an artwork lighter at the top than the bottom, it's better to use it with more horizontal pieces.

**Adjusting the Lights.** However you light your work, study the way the light strikes it critically. Adjust the angle of your light source—its height and horizontal position—so that it falls across the artwork in the most descriptive way. Determine how much shadow on the side opposite the light source is necessary to define the contour of the work. Think about where the shadow of the work itself falls on the background, because this will be a part of your final image, even if quite soft or light. If the shadow seems too long, raise the lights and angle them down more. If you feel the light is too flat, try a thinner diffusion material, or if bounce lighting, move the lights closer to your reflecting surface. Moving the light source farther away from the work will also accomplish this, but do so only if you can afford the loss in brightness. If you're using an umbrella with a white surface, consider exchanging it for one with a silver lining, which will give you a more contrasty, directional light. A similar alternative, if you're using a white card as a reflector, is to wrap aluminum foil around it, although you should make sure that it doesn't create a blotchy pattern. The effect of any of these techniques may not be fully apparent until you get your photographs back, at which time you may have to make the appropriate adjustments and reshoot the work. For this reason, it's wise to leave your setup intact until you get your film back.

**Filling in Shadows.** Reflectors can also be used to bounce the light from your main source, whether it's direct, bounced, or diffused, back into the shadowed portions of the work. A large, neutral white card or sheet, placed off-camera on the side of the work opposite the light, will "fill in" shadows that might otherwise be objectionably dark. Adjust the amount of fill by moving the card in and out until the relationship between the directly lighted parts of the work and the shadows looks right, remembering that photographic film won't always see things the way you do. Because your eye adjusts its "aperture" constantly for differences in brightness, they will tend to look more extreme in the finished slide. But by the same token, avoid over-filling the shadows, because this will reduce the sense of volume in the artwork. This is a particular risk in very light-surfaced works, which often need no fill light at all, if your main light source is soft enough and properly positioned. Darker works usually require heavier fill. The fill potential of your reflector can be increased by foil-wrapping it, but watch for spotty light.

If you exercise discretion, you can even use another light to fill in shadows. It must be much further away than your main light source, or much more heavily diffused or otherwise reduced in brightness (e.g., through use of a lower-wattage bulb), so that it doesn't create a second set of shadows. If kept at reduced strength, it can even be used on axis with the camera, with your main light coming strongly from the side. This is a traditional technique in photographic portraiture, in which the ideal relative brightness of the main light and fill light is said to be 3:1. Our approach will be somewhat more seat-of-

the-pants, but as we'll see, your camera's meter can be used to measure and establish this relationship.

Because of its soft quality, bounce lighting often permits the use of multiple light sources, even at distances from one another that might otherwise create double shadows. For example, if you have a relatively low white ceiling, you can place a light on either side of the camera and bounce them both against it. (Keep them high for greater efficiency, and to reduce the possibility of direct light spilling onto the artwork and setup.) This will produce a soft, almost shadowless, top light that is well suited to many kinds of work.

## FILM AND THREE-DIMENSIONAL WORK

Adding more light to any artwork will help you stick to reasonably fast shutter speeds and let you use relatively small apertures. But you may only have a bulb or two at your disposal, or want to light the work in such a way that using a second bulb will cause double shadows. If you are using bulbs color-rated for 3200 degrees Kelvin, you do have the option of using High-speed tungsten Ektachrome to achieve shorter exposures and/or enable you to use smaller apertures. This film is not quite as fine-grained as its ISO 50 cousin, which is why it's more appropriate for shooting work in existing tungsten light, such as in a gallery, than well-lighted individual works of art. But the difference is almost invisible unless the slide is printed or projected, and the film's extra speed may actually help you obtain better results in certain circumstances.

High-speed tungsten Ektachrome is over one-and-a-half times more sensitive to light than an ISO 50 film. This means that a picture you would have to take at a

shutter speed of one second with an aperture between f8 and f11, you could instead take at ½ second at f11.

**Push the Film.** Two other techniques may be used to obtain higher film "speed," but they generally won't yield as good results as a conventionally processed tungsten-balanced film. One is to "push" the film as explained in the section in chapter 7, on page 104. This entails setting an ISO higher than the one recommended for the film, to trick the meter into thinking that the film doesn't need as much exposure. This reduced exposure is then compensated for with extended development, but a by-product of the technique is increased contrast and graininess in the slide. High-speed Ektachrome is usually "pushed" to an ISO of 320, which allows you to use a one-stop faster shutter speed—¼ instead of ½ second, for example—or a smaller aperture, f16 instead of f11. Your camera's meter will indicate these changes when you reset the ISO.

The 3M Corporation, under the "Scotch" brand, makes a tungsten-balanced slide film with an impressive ISO of 640, giving it twice the effective speed even of High-Speed Ektachrome exposed for a one-stop push. In the example above, this would permit the use of yet a smaller aperture, or a faster shutter speed—f22 instead of f16, or ⅛ second instead of ¼. The price of this film's speed, however, is a very visible graininess.

**High-Speed Daylight Film.** Another way of obtaining somewhat higher film speed is to shoot one of the currently popular high-speed daylight-balanced color slide films—preferably with an ISO of 1600—and use a blue filter over the camera's lens to compensate for the warmth with which the film

## IMPORTANCE OF SHOOTING SEVERAL VIEWS OF A SCULPTURAL WORK

Unlike two-dimensional artwork, most three-dimensional work is meant to be seen from many different angles. Because a photograph doesn't give a curator or gallery director the opportunity to walk around your artwork, be sure to provide more than a single view of a three-dimensional piece.

interprets tungsten light. But the presence of the filter (the use of which is described on page 99, chapter 7) reduces the light entering the camera by two full stops. The effect of this is an exposure—i.e., a combination of aperture and shutter speed—equal to what a tungsten film with an ISO of 400 would yield, but with the huge grain size of an ultra-fast film.

**Kodachrome KPA.** If you're shooting Kodachrome KPA, and feel you should be using smaller apertures, the option of a higher-speed version of the film is not available to you, because no other film is balanced for the 3400-degree light of the bulbs you are using with it. Kodak will push this film one stop to an ISO of 80 (which you should remember to set before metering your work, if you opt for such special processing), allowing you to use a one-stop smaller aperture, but the service costs a hefty $9 (as of this writing) on top of the usual processing charge. Because of the limitations of Kodachrome KPA's speed and reciprocity characteristics, you may be better off using a tungsten film balanced for 3200 degrees K for three-dimensional work.

## METERING AND EXPOSING FILM
### CHOOSING A SHUTTER SPEED

The use of diffusion and bounce-lighting techniques will inevitably reduce the intensity of your tungsten bulbs. While you can always cluster more bulbs as long as they don't create double shadows, try to minimize this loss by keeping the light source as close to the artwork as possible without causing an uneven appearance, and by using as efficient a reflector or as thin a diffusion material as you can without compromising the quality of the light. Even so, three-dimensional

work will generally require slower shutter speeds than flat work. Don't be afraid to use them; your tripod will keep the camera steady. But read on to find out when you might encounter a problem.

If your camera is the sort that only offers shutter speeds of up to $1/8$ or $1/4$ second, you may be forced to use wider apertures than are preferable for three-dimensional work. You can, however, set the camera on "B," which keeps the shutter open for as long as the shutter button is depressed, and using a cable release, time the exposures with a watch. For accuracy, you will probably have to use shutter speeds of a second or longer, because the slower the speed, the less significant any error on your part will be. (A $1/4$ second error is only an eighth of a stop—12 percent—at a two-second shutter speed, but it's a half-stop—50 percent—at a $1/2$ second speed.) These timed speeds will allow you to use smaller lens apertures, just as if your camera offered the actual shutter settings. But for accuracy's sake, if your camera is limited in this respect, you may want to use additional light and/or a higher-speed film such as Ektachrome 160.

Most 35mm SLRs offer shutter speeds of at least a second, and some go up to thirty seconds. The increments on this whole-second side of the shutter speed range are similar to the fractional speeds—four, eight, fifteen, and thirty seconds—so don't get the two mixed up. They're usually color-coded differently on the dial, and displayed with a different symbol inside the viewfinder. But like the fractional speeds, any change in these slower shutter speeds represents a whole stop increase or decrease in exposure, a change that your camera's meter will at-

tempt to compensate for by choosing or recommending a different lens aperture.

**Shutter Speed and Reciprocity Failure.** For example, the meter will tell you that an eight-second exposure at f11 is the same as a fifteen-second exposure at f16, or that a four-second exposure at f11 is the same as a two-second exposure at f8. The problem with this is that the meter doesn't adjust for the increasing loss of sensitivity that photographic films experience at very slow shutter speeds, the reciprocity failure described in chapter 2. If you're shooting at shutter speeds of more than a couple of seconds (or slower than $1/8$ second with Kodachrome KPA) you will need to give the film some additional exposure beyond what the gray card indicates, to prevent the underexposure that reciprocity failure causes. Because at exposure times of less than ten seconds this correction usually amounts to a half-stop of extra exposure, you can accomplish it simply by bracketing your exposures more heavily on the "over" (plus) side. But if you bracket your exposures with the lens aperture, don't compromise your depth of field by using apertures that are too wide. And if you use the shutter, keep in mind that because of the film's increasing loss of sensitivity, a full stop change—say from four to eight seconds—may only net you a half-stop more effective exposure.

**Color Variation.** Reciprocity failure may also cause a slight change in color, another effect of very long exposures. High-speed Ektachrome may show a color change at shutter speeds slower than half a second; Ektachrome 50, on the other hand, shows little change even at exposure times of a minute, although exposure must be increased by about a stop at such times. Kodachrome KPA falls somewhere in between. Should such color shifts become a problem, they can be corrected with a filter over the camera lens. (Read the section on filters for further information, page 98.) The information sheet enclosed with these films will often recommend a specific filter for different long exposures, along with a suggested exposure increase at those times.

## CHOOSING AN APERTURE

All this about slower shutter speeds is by way of saying that you shouldn't let the loss of light that diffusion and bounce-lighting techniques cause force you to use wide lens apertures to obtain proper film exposure. Wide lens apertures reduce your depth of field—the zone of sharpness in the picture—and good depth of field is even more important in shooting three-dimensional work than it is with flat work.

If any general rule can be applied, use an aperture of at least f8, and if possible f11. But the right aperture is very much a function of the individual artwork. The deeper the artwork, for example, the smaller the aperture you will need to use to include all of it in the zone of sharpness. The smaller it is, the more depth of field you will need to make it sharp, because depth of field is much shallower *at the same aperture* when you focus your lens close. By the same token, details of a larger piece will also require the use of smaller apertures than the photographs of the entire piece. For details of small or deep works, an aperture as small as f16 is sometimes appropriate, light levels and shutter speeds permitting. Use of an aperture that is too wide for the artwork will result in parts of it appearing unsharp in the photograph.

A more precise method of determining what aperture is appropri-

ate to your artwork is to use the depth of field scale on your camera's lens barrel. This scale will tell you how deep your zone of sharpness will be at various apertures, and its use is described in detail in the box on pages 34 and 35 in chapter 2. You can see from the scale that where you focus has as much effect on a photograph's depth of field as your choice of aperture, and focusing properly can maximize your depth of field. Your first inclination may be to focus on the closest part of the artwork, but because the zone of sharpness any given aperture offers extends both in front of where you've focused as well as behind it, you will be throwing away the front portion of it if you do so. In fact, the zone of sharpness surrounding any point on which you focus extends about twice as far behind that point as it does in front of it. By this formula, if you focus about a third of the way between the closest and the farthest points you want to render sharply, then choose an aperture which will give you enough depth of field to include both points, you will have made the most of that aperture's depth of field.

**Don't Believe Your Eyes.** The only thing that may make you nervous about doing this is that, as seen through the lens, the front of the artwork in particular may appear to be somewhat out of focus. This will not, however, be the artwork's final appearance in the photograph. The camera keeps the lens open to its maximum aperture until just before you fire the shutter, in order to allow as much light into the viewfinder as possible so that you have a bright image to frame and focus. When you trip the shutter, the lens is automatically stopped down to the lens aperture you have set before the curtain opens. (If you are using a very old

camera, you may have to open and close the lens aperture manually for viewing and shooting.) One way to get a sense of the final appearance of the artwork is by depressing the camera's depth of field preview button, if it has one. This lets you view the subject at the aperture you have set the lens to, although it will darken the viewfinder considerably. While the subject will appear much sharper, this device should never be used as a substitute for the depth of field scale on the lens barrel; although something may look sharp in the viewfinder or even the final slide, it may not appear sharp in the projected slide or enlarged print.

As you begin to understand the way depth of field works, you'll realize that wider apertures give better depth of field when you're farther away from your subject. If your piece is large and fairly shallow, for example, you may be far enough away from it to get away with an aperture of f5.6.

## TAKING THE LIGHT READING

Once you've decided what aperture you need, you can use the gray card to determine the shutter speed you'll need in the light you have on the work. Take the camera carefully off the tripod. Place the gray card in the middle of the work so that the light falls on it unimpeded, and make it face the camera position. Since you will probably need two hands to operate the camera, you may want to secure the card in some way, or else have a friend hold it for you. Fill the camera viewfinder with the card, but make sure not to cast a shadow on it. (If a friend is holding it, be sure he or she doesn't cast a shadow either.) There's no need to focus the camera on the card.

At this point, an aperture-priority automatic camera will set a shutter speed automatically when you set the aperture you've chosen. With a shutter-priority automatic camera, you must adjust the shutter speed until your chosen aperture appears in the viewfinder display. In either case, you will probably have to override the camera's automatic exposure system when it comes time to make the actual exposures, to make it accept the settings indicated by the gray card reading. With a manually set camera, of course, you simply adjust the shutter speed until you match up the needle, get the right diode to glow, or see both plus and minus symbols in the viewfinder. The proper exposure is then locked in.

## EXPOSING FOR HIGHLIGHTS

You can also take gray card readings at various points on the work to be sure that more or less the same exposure is indicated in the highlighted areas. This isn't quite as critical as it is with flat work, and

softening the light by diffusing it or bouncing it tends to make it more broad and even to begin with. And of course, part of the modeling effect of light on three-dimensional work has to do with the way it changes in brightness across the artwork's surfaces. Pieces that are very tall, wide, or long do run some risk of being unevenly lighted, however, and if you take readings to check this, keep the gray card in direct light, in the plane of the particular surface of the artwork you are metering. A tall vertical piece, for example, should be metered top to bottom on its highlighted side.

**Test Case.** Let's say your first, central gray card reading of such a piece indicates an exposure of ½ second at f11. The reading you take at the top of the piece, however, indicates ½ second at f8, or one second at f11 (both the same exposure), telling you that the light there is a stop dimmer than that in

the middle. You either need to raise your light source, aim it up, or if these adjustments in turn reduce the light on the bottom of the work, back your light source away from the work to make it cover the work more evenly. This adjustment will reduce the light level overall, so take your central gray card reading again to determine the correct exposure.

Let's say your work is horizontal, and you've lighted it from the left side. You get a gray card reading from the middle of the work of one second at f16. But the reading you get on the right side of the work is one second at between f16 and f11, indicating the light there is a half-stop dimmer than that in the middle. (An aperture-priority automatic exposure system will probably display two seconds at f16, because it can only indicate whole shutter speeds, whether it is capable of actually using in-between ones or not.) In order to correct this, you can do one or more of several things.

You can reduce the angle at which the light strikes the artwork, bringing it closer to the camera so that it strikes the work more broadside. (This may reduce the sense of texture in the work, but there are always trade-offs.) You can back the light away from the work to make it more even, although this will mean using a wider aperture or slower shutter speed, as indicated by the camera when you take a new reading. Alternatively, you can try boosting the light level at the end of the piece by using a larger reflector (white sheet or board) to bounce some of the light back into the work.

## SHOOTING DETAILS

Sometimes an overall view of an artwork fails to convey its full richness, especially if it is never pro-

Metering 3-D art with the gray card.

jected or enlarged. If your work is large and/or complex, or if it has distinctive surface characteristics, you should consider shooting details of it to supplement the overall view. If you're not using a macro lens, or a zoom lens with a "macro" mode, shooting details often requires the use of close-up attachments. Read the section on shooting small work in chapter 7 for more details.

Because depth of field is reduced at the close distances involved in shooting details, you should use smaller lens f-stops. This will in turn require the use of slower shutter speeds to obtain equivalent exposure. If you boost the light levels, however, you may be able to use smaller f-stops without changing shutter speeds. (You can do this simply by moving your light source as close to the work as the need for evenness permits.) Anytime you change the light, of course (whether to brighten the artwork or alter the light's character and direction to suit a specific detail), you will have to take a new meter reading and change your camera's settings accordingly.

If you're still uncertain about how to determine the correct exposure, or how to override an automatic camera to obtain the correct exposure, review the section at the end of chapter 2. Chapter 2 also explains how to bracket your exposures with either an automatic or a manual camera. Bracketing your exposures is in some respects even more important with three-dimensional work than two-dimensional work, because of the greater range of brightnesses that unidirectional light is likely to create in the artwork. Be sure to use your cable release, and let the camera "settle" between exposures.

Finally, remember that you don't have to accept your first results, as you normally do when you hire a professional photographer. If you're unhappy with the quality and direction of the light, or the angle and presentation of the piece, you can always reshoot it for no more than the cost of another roll of film. If you've had a technical problem, however, refer to chapter 6, "Evaluating Your Results," for help in diagnosing it.

## VARIATIONS ON THREE-DIMENSIONAL WORK

The general principles outlined so far will apply to most kinds of three-dimensional artwork. But because it's impossible to address every variation of such work in the limited space of this book, you must experiment to arrive at a treatment suited to your specific work. If your work is environmental, or if it is difficult to photograph independent of its exhibition space, refer to the next chapter, on installation photography.

### METALLIC WORK

Other techniques, both in lighting and in presentation, may be useful in photographing three-dimensional work, particularly if it's reflective in nature. Metallic work, for example, must reflect something in order to appear shiny. The kind of broad, soft light that is appropriate to other three-dimensional artwork is also good for metallic work, but usually only as a starting point. You will have to augment it with reflectors, such as neutral white sheets or cards—matboard works well—propped up off-camera around the artwork. (For very large work, you may have to rob the linen closet.) Arrange the reflectors by inspection; keep looking through the camera's viewfinder as you reposition and reorient them, until any distractingly dark

areas in the piece are brightened. Keep the number of reflectors to a minimum, because a very shiny piece may reflect the seams or dark lines where they meet. By the time you're done, the artwork may be surrounded by a veritable wall of reflectors, with the camera's lens poking through it.

### OTHER SETUPS

Shiny three-dimensional work presents another problem. If you're shooting a standing piece against a curved background, its lower portions will often reflect the ground. If you're using a white ground and lighting a metallic piece with a tent or reflectors, this usually isn't a problem. But on a dark or colored ground it's a problem both for metallic work and other kinds of shiny work, such as high-glaze ceramics.

**Plexiglas.** The solution is to use clear Plexiglas as a background material, as mentioned earlier in the chapter. (If you're shooting against a flat background, as with jewelry, you can use a sheet of glass.) The Plexiglas must be large enough and flexible enough to substitute for the seamless, which you should roll out or place several feet behind the Plexiglas surface. You can't do this with an upright table, obviously, because you'll see the table and wall surfaces behind the Plexiglas. You'll need to turn the table on its side, with the top facing out toward your camera position and the legs pointing toward the wall. You can clamp the Plexiglas to the legs of the table (it will have to be roughly the same width as the table for you to do this), allowing it to curve up against the wall as if it were a seamless. Alternatively, you can use a couple of sawhorses, placing them perpendicular to the wall and running the outside edges of the horizontal part of the Plexiglas along each crosspiece. The

## OTHER SETUPS FOR THREE-DIMENSIONAL WORK

If you want to eliminate the shadow of your artwork, you can photograph it on a milky Plexiglas or a clear Plexiglas with a sheet of diffusion film or tracing vellum over it, and backlight it from below (top). This will, however, make the background virtually blank, and if not carefully controlled can reduce the sharpness of the edges of the work. An alternative to this, and one which permits the use of colored grounds, is to photograph the work on clear Plexiglas and roll out a seamless background paper below it (bottom). You may have to throw additional light on the seamless because of its increased distance from the light source. Either of these techniques requires that you turn the table you are working with on its side, as described in the text.

important thing is to have enough clearance behind the Plexiglas for the seamless or other background material, which must be at a reasonable distance from the Plexiglas for the technique to work, and to avoid a confusing shadow. Secure the upper edge of the seamless to the wall behind the Plexiglas, and let it drop at a steeper incline than the plexi, curving out smoothly beneath it.

**Reflection Control.** If the seamless or other background is fairly dark in color, the foreground Plexiglas may reflect the image of the work. This effect can be quite interesting, but if you don't like it you can minimize it by throwing additional light on the seamless to brighten it, baffling the light so that none of it spills onto the piece. It's not a bad idea to throw extra light on the seamless anyway, so that it will register as a bright, even tone. Don't overdo it, though; a colored ground should rarely be more than a couple of stops brighter than your gray card reading. The additional light shouldn't affect your meter reading if you take the reading in the usual way, making sure to keep stray light out of the lens.

You may also be able to cut out some of the reflection of an artwork on a clear Plexiglas surface with a polarizing filter. Mount the filter on the lens, and turn its rotating ring until the reflection disappears or is most fully subdued in the viewfinder. As always, be sure to have the filter on the lens when you take your gray card readings. It will, because it cuts back the light reaching the film, force you to use slower shutter speeds or wider apertures to obtain proper exposure. Refer to the section on filters in chapter 7 for further information about this filter.

If you want to combine the technique described above with tent lighting, you're undertaking a very complex setup, even by professional standards. But it's often the ideal technique for artwork such as silver and jewelry, because it allows you to use a darker background for heightened contrast and better definition of the shape of a piece.

## TRANSILLUMINATION

The clear Plexiglas-dropped seamless technique is also quite effective in eliminating the shadow of an artwork, whether on a white or a darker or colored ground. As mentioned, the seamless or other background must be far enough away from the Plexiglas and the artwork so that any shadow cast on it will fall out of the picture area. But you can also eliminate shadows by transilluminating, or backlighting, the surface that the artwork sits on. The surface must be translucent for this to work, and you will have to turn your table on its side as previously described, to leave enough space underneath for even lighting.

The ideal material for a transilluminated background is a sheet of translucent (milky) Plexiglas. But if you have a piece of clear Plexiglas already, you can place a large sheet of diffusion film or heavy tracing vellum on it to make it translucent. A sheet of glass can be used to support these materials in a shoot-down setup. If you need a curved background, but don't have either kind of Plexiglas, try placing a sheet of glass across the legs of your table to support the artwork, and run a sheet of diffusion film across it and up the wall, curving it as if it were a seamless. Some diffusion films may be stiff enough to hold a light artwork without any underlying support, but make sure the work doesn't distort the film by its weight.

**Even Illumination.** Again, you will need to leave enough room under your translucent ground to illuminate it evenly. Particularly if you are using a relatively large, curved background, this may require the use of two lights, probably of lower wattage than the 500s you will be using to light the work itself. Careful metering of the front surface of the background will help you make the light both even and of the correct intensity. Don't overilluminate the background; it should be no more than three or four stops brighter than your gray card reading, depending on whether you want to tone down or eliminate the shadows completely. If the backlighting is too strong, it may cause fogging of the artwork, or halation (the formation of a halo) around its edges. This technique will, however, produce a more or less blank background.

One advantage to this technique is that multiple light sources can be used without creating confusing double shadows.

In general, the larger the piece, the bigger the reflectors will have to be, but their size and position will also depend on the contours and surface characteristics of the piece. A piece that curves away from the camera, or that has a hammered surface, may require more reflectors on the side than a flatter, smoother piece. When larger metallic works require that the reflectors be placed at a significant distance from the piece, their effectiveness is reduced, and you may have to throw light back into the reflectors with additional bulbs. In fact, some pieces may be better served by bouncing light directly into the reflectors, regardless of their size. If you do this, be sure that no light enters the lens directly; baffle the lens if need be.

Lighting reflective work effec-

## TENT LIGHTING

Highly reflective sculpture with a mirror-like finish will need to be photographed completely surrounded by a translucent tent to eliminate the environment. Construct the tent from thin white fabric such as sail cloth or a commercial diffusion film once you have established your camera position so that it extends all the way from the camera to the edges of your background material. Tack or tape it to the edges of the table you're shooting on.

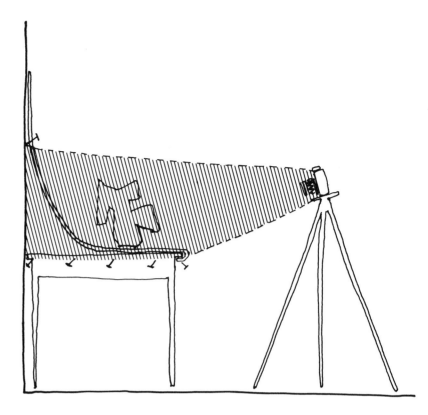

tively involves striking a delicate balance. Work that reflects too much light too uniformly loses a sense of surface and volume in the photograph. Should this happen, or if you suspect it may happen, you can even substitute light gray reflectors for white ones, to reduce their reflectivity. Metal surfaces that are worked—whether hammered, sandblasted, or etched—scatter the light they reflect, solving many of these problems.

## TENT LIGHTING

Work that is highly polished and smooth, on the other hand, is much more difficult to photograph. It acts as a mirror, reflecting camera, tripod, reflectors, and the light source itself. Although it may sometimes be successfully lighted with a carefully placed light source and reflecting cards virtually surrounding it, more often than not you must build a translucent tent around it to completely eliminate the environment it would otherwise reflect.

**Tent Materials.** Various kinds of thin white fabric can be used for a light tent, provided they transmit light readily. (Because they don't, bedsheets are unsuitable.) Fabrics with some "give" can be pulled taut to produce a smooth inner surface. White sailcloth is an excellent and relatively inexpensive tenting material, when you can find it. Sailmakers may sell you the ends of rolls; buy it in a lighter weight for greater translucency.

Neutral white plastic bags can also be used, but don't let their seams or the places you tape them together be reflected in the piece. A more professional approach is to purchase a commercial diffusion film from a photography dealer, either by the running foot or the roll. (Cloth-like materials are also available.) Ask which weight is a satisfactory compromise between good diffusing properties and efficient light transmission. The nature of the material you choose for your tent will depend in part on its size.

**Pitching the Tent.** Don't construct your tent until you've established your camera position, because the latter will determine the size of the tent. Whether you're shooting your artwork against a flat or curved background, you will need to make the tent extend all the way from the camera to the edges of your background material. Tack it or tape it to the edges of the table you're shooting on, or to the floor. You will probably have to extend the material above the piece as well, unless its surfaces are strictly vertical. Cut a small slit or hole in the material to poke the lens through.

You may have to construct a framework of sorts to support the tenting material, using wooden dowels or other rigid rods. Remember, though, that any material inside the tent may be reflected by the piece. Commercial diffusion film may be rigid enough to support itself, in small enough sheets.

In spite of the tent, if you're shooting a very shiny, frontal artwork you may see the reflection of the lens when you look through the camera. It will appear as a dark spot in the middle of the piece.

Photographing from a different angle may eliminate the spot, but may not represent the piece to your liking. Professional large-format cameras with independently moving backs can be used to prevent the effect, but in 35mm photography, it is inevitable. When all else fails, it may be possible to airbrush it out professionally for reproduction.

**Lighting the Tent.** Once you've constructed your tent, experiment with the position of the light or lights. Careful placement can mean the difference between a metallic artwork that appears flat and washed out and one that looks shiny, without distracting reflections. Lighting the tent from one side may create more of a shadow on the far side of the piece, helping to preserve its sense of volume. Lighting from the top is a way of avoiding hot spots in a piece with mostly vertical surfaces. Be careful, as always, not to get your bulbs too close to the tenting material, to avoid melting or setting fire to it.

If you use your imagination, you may be able to improvise on the tent theme. Lampshades, large translucent plastic food containers or bottles (cut a strategic hole in them for the camera lens), and the like may be used for smaller objects such as jewelry, particularly if you plan to "shoot down" on them.

A professional shortcut in photographing a highly polished object is to use a commercial dulling spray. It's sold in an aerosol can and is often made by the same companies that manufacture spray-on fixatives. The spray is easily wiped off, provided there aren't a lot of nooks and crannies for it to get trapped in. However, dulling spray can alter the apparent surface characteristics of a piece, making its high polish look almost sandblasted. Use it only as a last resort.

## SUMMARY/**THREE-DIMENSIONAL WORK**

- The quality of light required to photograph three-dimensional work should ordinarily be softer than the direct light appropriate for two-dimensional work.
- The light from tungsten photoflood bulbs may be softened by bouncing or diffusing it. A photographic umbrella permits controlled bounce lighting; a white plastic bag or shower curtain makes a good diffuser.
- Three-dimensional work is usually photographed against a seamless background. The seamless can be of many different materials, but should be of a color or tone that creates good contrast between the artwork and background.
- Telephoto lenses, or zoom lenses set to longer-than-50mm focal lengths, may prevent distortion of the artwork.
- Attach your background material to the wall behind your working surface. It should be of adequate width to fill the viewfinder frame when the camera is at shooting distance.
- Roll out the background so that it forms a gentle curve on its way to the surface where the artwork will sit. The horizontal portion should be at least as generous as the vertical. Cut the length off and secure it to the working surface.
- Place the artwork on the horizontal part of the seamless, making sure it's not too close to where the seamless begins to curve up. Turn it so that the side you want to photograph is facing out.
- Set the camera and tripod at a distance from the work at which it fills the frame. (Don't, however, make it uncomfortably tight.) Adjust the camera height to suit the work.
- Light the work in a way that best describes its shape, contours, and textures. With many three-dimensional works, this involves a single soft light source above and to the front and side of the work. Be conscious of how the shadow of the work falls on the ground, as well as of how the light falls on the work itself.
- If the shadows the work casts on itself (especially the shadow on the side opposite the light source) are too dark, fill them in by placing a white reflector off-camera nearby.
- Making sure your camera's film speed dial is set to the proper ISO for the film you are using, take a gray card reading at the work to determine the proper exposure.
- When you take the reading, select an aperture small enough to provide depth of field adequate to encompass the depth of the work. Use the shutter speed needed to obtain proper exposure at this aperture.
- To appear shiny, metallic work must have something light to reflect. This may be just a few strategically placed white cards, or involve the construction of a translucent tent around the work.
- If metallic or other shiny artwork reflects the color of the background material it sits on, replace the seamless with a sheet of Plexiglas and run the seamless beneath it. (This will require turning your table on its side to create an open area under the Plexiglas.)
- To eliminate the shadow of an artwork, shoot it either on clear Plexiglas with the seamless background underneath, or on a translucent background material that can be lighted from behind.

Many artists like to keep a photographic record of their exhibitions. Installed, an artist's work takes on a presence that photographs of individual pieces often don't convey. For this reason, you may even wish to include an installation view or two with a group of slides you submit to a gallery, to give the curator a better sense of how your work might appear on his or her walls.

For some artists, the installation is the only occasion on which the work is whole. This is certainly true for artists who do sculptural work that depends on its specific space for structural and aesthetic support. It's also true for environmental artists, for whom the installation and the artwork are one and the same. Even conceptual work, in the absence of a physical "piece," depends on a gallery display for its form. For artists working in these areas, good photographs of work on exhibition are all the more imperative.

Although it's hard to generalize about such a broad range of potential subject matter and locations, the technique involved in installation photography is really more akin to that of conventional photography than to the photography of individual works of art. It's usually better, for example, to accept the existing light on installed artwork because of the difficulty involved in lighting large spaces realistically. And in adding your own artificial light to an installation, you may create discrepancies in color temperature, particularly if you are shooting with natural light and daylight film.

Whether you're shooting inside or out, think about the relationship of your work to its environment, and compose your photograph carefully. Remember that your three-dimensional view of the exhibition or installation will be reduced to a flat image, in which spatial information must be conveyed by two-dimensional cues. In photographing outdoor installations, avoid confusing backgrounds; in shooting an exhibition, avoid compositions in which sculptural objects and paintings overlap. Choose angles from which the components of the installation will be clearly separated—for example, from which a piece of sculpture in the foreground can be "placed" against an empty wall between two paintings. If this kind of separation can't be achieved by a lateral movement of the camera, you may have to shoot from a higher angle, if your tripod has enough extension. (Use a stool or stepladder to look through the viewfinder.)

Suppress your more artful instincts in shooting installation views. Don't compose in such a way as to distract from the work on display.

## WORK INSTALLED OUTDOORS

If your work is installed outdoors, your task is a relatively simple one. Remember to use daylight, not tungsten film. Unless the light is very low and/or you can't use a tripod, choose a film of modest speed for its higher sharpness and finer grain: ISO 50, 64, or 100 slide films, ISO 100 or 125 print films. Try to get a sense of how your work appears at different times of day and in different weather conditions, to establish what kind of light is most appropriate or flattering to it. It could be that bright, direct sunlight, seemingly the obvious

Courtesy Grossman Gallery, Boston Museum School.

## IMPORTANCE OF CAMERA POSITION

In shooting either indoor or outdoor views of an installed work or an exhibition, place your camera so that foreground and background elements don't overlap in a distracting way. The bottom view suffers from a lack of balance; most of the artworks are bunched up on the left. The top view is a more balanced composition. The difference between a clean and a confusing installation view may involve an adjustment in camera position of as little as a couple of feet. In general, avoid cropping artworks. Artwork on display is usually better served by quiet, classical composition.

choice, interrupts its continuity by throwing some parts of it into deep shadow and highlighting other areas. You may prefer to shoot by the gentler, raking light of a late afternoon or early morning sun, which enhances textures, throws long shadows, and produces an attractive warmth. Even the suffused light of dawn or dusk, just before or after the sun rises or sets, can give three-dimensional work a sense of volume and wholeness that direct light may not. This is also true of the broad, soft light of an overcast day. If you do choose either of the latter options, you may want to put a warming filter on the camera to correct the blue cast that slides shot at these times of day can acquire. Either an 81A or 81B filter, both available in glass, is best for this.

While the higher shutter speeds outdoor light permits often make it possible to dispense with a tripod, it's not a bad idea to use one anyway. Using a tripod eliminates your own unsteadiness as a variable should your pictures come out unsharp, and perhaps more importantly, it tends to make you compose more carefully, to think harder about what points of view most cleanly and interestingly represent the artwork. You can also use slower shutter speeds than you could by handholding the camera, should you want to use smaller lens apertures for better depth of field, particularly when using films with lower sensitivity to light. This might well be a consideration in photographing a work that extends over a large area, especially if you choose to photograph it in low light. The improved depth of field available at smaller apertures also opens up the possibility of creating interesting relationships between near and far elements of your work, in that it enables you to keep both sharp. Remember to maximize your depth of field by careful focusing, as described in chapter 2, and in the box on reading your lens' depth of field scale on pages 34 and 35.

## LENSES AND OUTDOOR INSTALLATIONS

A wide-angle lens, if available, will provide better depth of field than a normal lens, although you will have to get closer to the artwork to make it fill the frame. It will also give a better sense of the setting of an artwork, because it allows you to make the piece fill the frame without cutting out as much of the background as a normal lens will. On the other hand, it may cause some artworks to appear attenuated from front to back, or cause the closest parts of the work to seem unnaturally prominent. With sprawling, large-scale works, outside or in, this effect may even prove to be a problem with a 50mm lens, in which event you may choose to use a telephoto lens. The greater camera-to-subject distance required by a telephoto lens causes an apparent compression in the subject, bringing its elements back into a relative scale that appears more natural.

## INTERIOR INSTALLATIONS

Inside, the requirements of installation photography are quite different. Although it's still advisable to shoot by available light, because of its reduced brightness you will almost invariably need to use a tripod, as well as "faster" films such as Kodak's High-Speed Ektachromes—ISO 160 for tungsten light, ISO 200 for daylight. If the light is exceptionally bright, you may be able to use the slower versions of these films—ISO 50 and 64 or 100—but never use tungsten Kodachrome (KPA) in an artificial-

Ralph Helmick

## EFFECT OF LENS FOCAL LENGTH ON OUTDOOR INSTALLATION VIEWS

It may seem unnecessary to use a wide-angle lens when you have unlimited space in which to photograph an artwork installed outdoors, but it often gives a better sense of the environment of the piece. The top picture was taken with a 50mm lens; notice how distractingly prominent the background elements are. In the bottom picture, taken from a closer position with a wide-angle lens, the artwork is the same size, if not larger, but the background elements have been reduced in size, and more of the immediate environment can be seen, including the entire bench at left.

ly lighted interior. It will render the light too warm.

For black and white prints, choose an ISO 400 film unless the light is very good, in which case you can sometimes use ISO 125. If you want prints from color negatives, you will be limited by the need to use a heavy blue filter on the lens, to compensate for the way these daylight-balanced films "see" tungsten light. The filter will cut back the light available to the film by two stops, reducing the effective speed of an ISO 400 film to ISO 100. For suggestions and a more detailed explanation, refer to the specific sections on making prints and using filters in chapter 7. If you're shooting installation views in artificial tungsten light, you should really have your prints made from tungsten-balanced slide films.

Even if the artwork in an exhibition area is lighted with tungsten spotlights, *don't* use a tungsten-balanced slide film if there is any significant natural light present; the film will see that part of the light as an objectionable blue color. In fact, even daylight film may pick up a bluish cast in daylighted areas of an inside installation, due to the blueness of the light from the windows, which is produced by open sky on a sunny day. A warming filter such as those described in chapter 7 may eliminate this, but it will make work that's lighted directly and strongly by gallery spotlights appear even warmer than daylight film alone would render it. (Avoid using daylight film to shoot strongly gallery-lighted individual works under these circumstances; better to shoot at night with tungsten film.)

## WAIT UNTIL DARK
In fact, unless the daylight in an exhibition space is particularly flattering to the installation, or if large

windows are an integral part of the space, it's better to shoot at night, by the gallery's artificial light alone. If you do this, or if no daylight is present in the space during the day, then use a tungsten-balanced film. Keep in mind, though, that because regular gallery lighting tends to be of slightly warmer color temperature than the 3200 degree light for which tungsten films are balanced, it will be rendered somewhat more warm by the film than the light from the color-rated bulbs that you would use to photograph individual works of art. Sticklers may choose to use a cooling filter over the lens, such as an 82 or 82A, to reduce the warmth of the result. Others may like it, feeling that it accurately represents the more golden cast of artificial light. And absolute color fidelity is less of an issue in installation photography anyway.

**Fluorescent Light.** In less well-appointed exhibition spaces, you may have to contend with fluorescent lights. If tungsten light or daylight is the principal light source, be sure to turn the fluorescents off; otherwise, they may create a greenish cast in the slide or color print. If fluorescents are the principal light source, though, you must use a magenta filter on the camera to eliminate the greenish cast. Because this filter, described below, will turn other kinds of light pink, you must block them out or turn them off. Also, because the light produced by garden-variety cool-white fluorescents is closer in color temperature to daylight than tungsten light, use daylight film to photograph under fluorescents. A fluorescent light's type is printed on the end of the tube, and each type requires a different color filter correction to appear "normal" on film. (See the chart in the "Filters" section of chapter 7, for specific infor-

mation, and page 110 for examples of the effects of fluorescents on color.)

Many glass filter manufacturers make a filter that they claim corrects cool white fluorescent light so that daylight film "sees" it normally, but sometimes these aren't quite strong enough. Cool white fluorescents are quite effectively corrected, however, with a Wratten CC 30 Magenta filter, available in a square optical gelatin from Kodak, or in glass from some other manufacturers. The glass filter will be the same price and much more durable, so buy it if you have the choice.

The simplest piece of advice is to avoid shooting under fluorescent light unless absolutely necessary. In addition to causing color variations, its quality is usually very unflattering.

## LENSES AND INTERIOR INSTALLATION VIEWS
Particularly in shooting an indoor exhibition, you may find that your 50mm lens seriously limits how much work you can include in your photographs. Even with your back against the far wall, its relatively narrow angle of view—so well-suited to shooting individual works—isn't wide enough to give a real sense of the scope of the show, of the relationships between its parts. If it's available to you, or if you're willing to rent one, a wide-angle lens will encompass a much larger part of an interior space than a 50mm lens, from the same point of view. Even a 35mm moderate wide-angle, while better than the 50mm in this respect, can be limiting; it's better to use a 28mm or 24mm lens. Lenses with wider angles of view than 24mm should be avoided, because of the distortion they're likely to cause. The new wide-angle zoom lenses can be useful in installation photography;

Courtesy Grossman Gallery, Boston Museum School.

## EFFECT OF LENS FOCAL LENGTH ON INTERIOR INSTALLATION VIEWS

A wide-angle lens is particularly useful in photographing exhibitions in small spaces. Both views above were taken from the same position, but the top photograph was shot with a 50mm "normal" lens, the bottom one with a 24mm wide-angle lens. The camera was as far away as possible, but the wide-angle lens affords a much fuller view of the exhibition.

they allow you to pick and choose the lens' angle of view at will, and you can use the narrowest angle that any given view requires, to keep distortion at a minimum. In other words, get as far away from the work as the view you want to shoot will allow, then zoom to the focal length setting that covers it. Keep in mind, though, that the closer shooting position afforded by a wide-angle lens gives more of a feeling in the photograph of being surrounded by the show, rather than looking at it from afar.

There are several visual by-products—some might call them drawbacks—of the wide-angle lens' ability to "see" a larger area. One is that it makes an interior seem bigger than it really is. (This effect usually seems more exaggerated in the camera viewfinder than in the finished slide, partly because you can compare it to the real thing.) The perspective conveyed by horizontal lines seems more forced, and foreground objects seem larger in relation to background objects. This effect is only detrimental when it causes foreground objects to begin to overlap the background.

**Perspective Distortion.** Another effect of the wide-angle lens should be more closely watched, because it can be controlled. This is that if the camera isn't kept level, i.e., so that the film plane is parallel to the vertical lines in the image, the lens will make those lines appear to lose their parallelism to each other. This effect is a more extreme version of the distortions you are attempting to correct when squaring up flat artwork. If the lens and camera are tipped upward, for example, vertical lines will converge toward the top of the image; if the lens and camera are tipped down, the lines will converge toward the bottom. This can

Courtesy Grossman Gallery, Boston Museum School.

## CORRECTION OF VERTICALS IN INTERIOR INSTALLATION VIEWS

One side effect of the wide-angle lens' better coverage is exaggerated perspective. This is usually only distracting when it causes vertical lines to be skewed. To avoid this effect, shown in the top photograph, keep the camera level, so that the film itself is parallel to the vertical lines in the subject. This often requires that the height of the camera be lowered, as in the bottom photograph. There may, however, be times when a higher camera position provides a clearer overview of the work on display, making the divergence of verticals a worthwhile trade-off.

be a distracting effect, and can distort the shapes of the artwork, especially on the edges of the image. It can happen to a lesser degree with a 50mm lens as well, so make a real effort to keep the camera level. A carpenter's bubble level or an angle finder can be useful for this.

Once you've leveled your camera, if you want to include more at the top of the image, rather than point the camera up, raise the tripod or its center column. If there's too much at the top, lower the camera rather than aiming it down. Your views needn't always be shot at eye-height.

Keeping the camera level may, at times, force you to include more of a pipe-filled ceiling or inelegant cement floor than you would like. The excess can always be masked out on the finished slide with opaque tape, or cropped or trimmed in a print, as described in chapter 7. If this isn't an option, you feel that the ceiling or floor is too distracting, and lowering or raising the camera position makes the viewpoint too extreme, you may decide to allow a little distortion of verticals. There are trade-offs in any such shooting situation. If you think a high-angle view of the installation makes the most interesting, informative photograph, then you will have to accept the divergence of verticals toward the top of the image that this will cause. Special lenses called "perspective-correcting" lenses are designed to eliminate this kind of distortion. They do this by enabling the lens to slide in its mount parallel to the camera body, so as to include more or less of the ceiling or floor while keeping the camera level. So-called "PC" lenses are extremely expensive, however, and smaller dealers may have to special-order them.

**Depth of Field.** Another argument for using a wide-angle lens in indoor installation photography is that at a given aperture and focused distance, its depth of field is greater than that of a normal lens. This is a real advantage at the closer shooting distances involved in installation photography, at which depth of field is shallower with any lens. Nevertheless, whether you're using a 50- or 24mm lens, you should select reasonably small apertures whenever possible, especially if you want to show both very close and more distant works clearly. Use the depth of field scale on your lens barrel to determine how deep your zone of sharpness will be at a given lens aperture. Don't hesitate to use slow shutter speeds if use of a smaller aperture makes them necessary in obtaining adequate exposure, but keep the characteristics of the film you're using in mind. Remember, too, that you will maximize your depth of field at a given aperture by focusing about a third of the way into your subject.

## SHUTTER SPEED AND INTERIOR INSTALLATIONS

The low light levels usually involved in interior installation photography will require the use of slower shutter speeds to obtain adequate exposure. The tripod will permit these by eliminating the possibility of camera movement, but any moving figures in your installation view will blur. Although this can be an interesting effect, it's not entirely controllable, and you have two other options: one, to shoot when there are no people in the scene (you may have to arrange to work when the gallery is closed to the public), and two, to ask any visitors to stand still when you make your exposures. You can also plant some friends in the view. Which you prefer is a matter of

Courtesy Massachusetts Artists Foundation

## EFFECT OF DEPTH OF FIELD ON INSTALLATION VIEWS

It's usually best to maximize depth of field in an installation view, as in the top photograph, by using a reasonably small lens aperture. This will make all the artworks in the view as sharp as possible. But there may be occasions when you want to single out your artwork, such as in a group show. You can do this by focusing on the piece, and using a wide aperture to cause the background to be out of focus, as in the bottom photograph. This reduced depth of field requires that you focus even more carefully.

taste: some like the spareness of an unpopulated installation view; others think it looks too sterile.

## EXPOSING FOR GALLERY LIGHT

Determining proper exposure for gallery light is trickier than exposing for the controlled light you've used in shooting individual works. It tends to be uneven, often much brighter on the work itself than in the surrounding areas. If you let your camera's light meter determine exposure based on the overall scene, it will average these darker surrounding areas into its reading, and recommend or set a combination of aperture and shutter speed that will cause the artworks to be overexposed—that is, too light—in the slide. For this reason, you should take your readings in the light falling on the artworks themselves, following the same procedure that you used in photographing individual works with your own lights.

Hold your 18 percent gray card in the light falling on a prominent piece, or an important part of a large-scale work. If it's a painting or a framed work, hold or secure the card in the plane of the work; if it's sculptural, keep it roughly vertical, depending on the orientation of the piece's major planes. Avoid angling the card toward any light source, whether window or spotlight, or you may get a false reading from the resulting glare. Fill your camera's viewfinder frame with the card. There's no need to focus on the card.

The camera will indicate the correct starting exposure for your installation view. If you've forgotten your gray card, either look for a value in the work that corresponds to a medium gray, and take your reading off it, or (if your skin color is light) take a reading off the flat of your hand, then increase exposure

by one stop to obtain the correct reading. You can either use a one-step slower shutter speed or a one-stop wider aperture, depending on where these controls have been set and the suggested shutter-speed range of the film.

**Manual vs. Automatic.** If your camera is manual, simply leave it set as is, mount it back on the tripod, and start shooting, ignoring the camera's probable indication that your picture will be underexposed. If you're using a camera that sets the shutter speed, the aperture, or both automatically, the camera will attempt to reset itself when you present it with your original composed view. You should override it, and there are several ways to do so, depending on the features your camera offers. One is to lock in the exposure with the "memory" or exposure lock provision when you're reading off the gray card, but for reasons explained in earlier chapters this may be somewhat awkward. It is nearly impossible and ill-advised if it requires holding in a button until the shutter is tripped.

You can also override the exposure by adjusting the exposure compensation dial, or, if your camera doesn't have one, the film speed (ISO) control. Once you've remounted the camera on a tripod, and recomposed the scene, adjust either control until the correct exposure—that is, the combination of shutter speed and aperture indicated by the gray card reading—is displayed in the camera's viewfinder. This adjustment will most often require turning the exposure compensation dial toward the minus side, or the ISO ring toward the higher numbers. This causes the camera to give the film less exposure than it would have based on an average reading, compensating for the overexposure that the darker

areas of the view might otherwise cause. But on some occasions, you may need to make these adjustments in the direction of overexposure. For a more detailed explanation of overriding an automatic camera, refer to chapters 2 and 3.

**Spot Readings.** Some newer cameras will allow you to take a "spot" reading off a very small area of your subject from far away. This might eliminate the need to remove the camera from the tripod to take light readings. If the spot reading is calibrated for the 18 percent reflectance of the gray card, be sure you place the "spot" in the viewfinder either on the gray card in the light falling on the artworks, or on a middle-gray tone of one of them. If the spot reading is based on highlight or shadow values, it becomes less reliable, but either a white area in one of the works or the white backside of the gray card can be used for a highlight reading, a black tone in one of the works for a shadow reading.

If the light levels on the various artworks in your installation view are radically different, you may have to average them together to determine a starting exposure, and some pieces will end up lighter or darker than others, even in a properly exposed slide. Take gray card readings in the center of each piece in the view you want to shoot, then use the median reading for your starting exposure, or split the difference. If one painting needs an exposure of ½ second at f11, another ½ second at f8, and a third ½ second at f5.6, start with ½ second at f8. If the light on most of the work is fairly consistent, but a few pieces are more brightly or dimly lighted, choose an exposure that favors most of the work.

Whatever your starting exposure, you should bracket it heavily, as described in the section on film exposure and in the chapters on two- and three-dimensional work. With a manually controlled camera, this involves changing the aperture and/or the shutter speed; with an automatic camera, it means adjusting the exposure-override control or resetting the ISO dial.

## OTHER LIGHTING CONSIDERATIONS

Another situation to avoid or be wary of is an interior installation in which portions are directly sunlit. The difference in brightness between the sunlit and ambient light-illuminated areas will be too great for the film to accommodate; depending on how the film is exposed, the sunlit parts will be washed out, the ambient light-illuminated parts too dark, or both. If the sunlit portions are nothing more than small patches on the floor, having them blank may be acceptable, although you should avoid taking averaged light readings that might be thrown off by them. But if the sunlit areas are large, important parts of the installation, you should wait for a time of day when the light on the exhibition is largely indirect.

## SUMMARY/**EXHIBITION PHOTOGRAPHY**

- A photographic record of your exhibitions may make an impressive and useful addition to a set of slides of your work (or other supporting materials) that you plan to submit to a gallery.
- Installation views should be composed with the same care and visual thought that you invest in your own artwork. Use a tripod; it aids in composition, and permits slow shutter speeds in the low light typical of exhibition spaces.
- A wide-angle lens is very useful in shooting installation views. Inside, it lets you include more of the exhibition when limited space won't let you get far enough away; outside, it can subdue a confusing environment, giving the work an extra prominence.
- When using a wide-angle lens, particularly in inside installations with vertical lines, try to keep the camera back as vertical as good composition permits.
- In most cases, exhibitions should be photographed using the light they are illuminated with. If the installation is lighted entirely or partially with daylight, use daylight film; if it's lighted with tungsten light, use tungsten film.
- If the lighting in an interior exhibition is a difficult mix of daylight and tungsten light, you may want to shoot after dark, when tungsten light is the only source and you can safely use tungsten-balanced film.
- If cool white fluorescent light is the principal light source, eliminate all other light and shoot daylight film with a CC 30 Magenta color correction filter.
- Depth of field is just as important in shooting an exhibition as it is in photographing an individual work of art. Use relatively small apertures to make sure that both the closest and farthest parts of the show are sharp. (Refer to the lens' depth of field scale for guidance.)
- To determine a starting exposure for an interior installation view, take a meter reading off the gray card, holding it in the light falling on a prominent work. If the light on the artworks varies greatly, take readings at several works and split the difference.
- If your camera is automatic, once you have established the gray card reading and recomposed your view, adjust its exposure to match the settings indicated by the gray card.
- Because installation views may include areas of considerably different brightness, bracket your exposures heavily.

No. 81A

KEEP IN A COOL DRY PL

Kodak
Wratten
gelatin filter

mm x 75 mm

CAT

No. 81B

KEEP IN A COOL DRY PLACE

Kodak
Wratten
gelatin filter

75 mm x 75 mm

CAT 149 6074

KEEP IN A COOL DRY PLACE

Kodak
color
compensating
filter

75 mm x 75 mm

1E5

CAT 149 6678

Have your film processed by a professional lab or a reputable photo finishing service. The energy you've invested in photographing your artwork is worth far more than the money you might save by patronizing a cut-rate or back-alley processing outfit. A good lab or photo finisher takes pains to ensure that the color of your slides will be true and consistent from one processed batch to the next, by running tests at regular intervals. It keeps its chemicals fresh, its machinery clean so that it won't scratch your film, and will mount your slides straight, so that your efforts at framing, centering, or squaring up won't be cancelled out. If your slides come back off-color, mottled, scratched, or cockeyed, the processing and "finishing" may be at fault, although even a good lab will make a mistake from time to time. For a more detailed explanation of the sorts of problems you're likely to encounter, and what to expect from the photo lab, read on.

Do a little shopping for a lab or photo finisher, and not just for price, which can vary considerably. Professional labs will charge more than most photo finishing services, but the difference—perhaps a dollar per roll for slides—may be worth the individual attention your film will get, and often buys you technical advice as well. Many professional labs specialize in slide processing, while most photo finishers make their money in the snapshot end of the trade, and may not treat your film as well. Often they will send it to another facility, where it is entirely out of their control.

## BLACK AND WHITE PROCESSING

Black and white processing and finishing, now the poor cousin of the industry, is an altogether different story. Even a professional lab that does excellent color work may commit mayhem with your roll of black and white film. Because there has been relatively little demand for commercial black and white work, the standards for it are much lower. The film is often processed in machines that haven't been well maintained, in chemicals that haven't been properly replenished. It frequently comes back underdeveloped, underfixed, and scratched. Given the choice, you may be better off sending your film to Kodak than trusting it to a color-oriented professional lab. But the best approach is to take or send the film to a lab that specializes in black and white work (such labs are appearing in growing numbers in major cities), where it will be processed with care and printed with the special understanding required.

## HOW LONG WILL IT TAKE?

Let the lab or photo finisher know that you've got important film to process, film which you went to a lot of trouble with to insure proper color and exposure. If they sense you'll be a stickler, and fear their results might not be up to your standard, they may point you elsewhere. If you really want to give them pause, ask how often they run a color test on their E-6 line—a reference to the standard processing chemistry and procedure for all the tungsten-balanced films described in this book, with the exception of Kodachrome KPA, which still must be sent to Kodak for processing.

If you're in the habit of using one-hour photo finishers for your snapshot processing, you may find that these facilities can't do on-premises slide processing, and send their slide film elsewhere to be processed. This can slow the turnaround time to several days. Kodak's high-quality slide processing, for example, whether of its Kodachrome or Ektachrome films, usually takes two days from a major city, longer from more remote outposts. Take your film to a lab or photography store that has a Kodak "rush" bag, and ask the clerk to put your film in it; sometimes you can get it back in a day, provided you make the daily pickup, although Kodak makes no guarantees for this free service. Don't leave your film at a drugstore or other photo drop that's likely to keep it sitting around for extended periods. Remember that careless storage can have an adverse effect on film color. Prepaid mailers (to which there may be no alternative in remote areas) put your film at risk in transit, since it gets handled like any other mail, and could spend a good part of its trip toasted by a mail truck's differential.

**Rush Service.** By contrast to most photo finishing services, a professional photo lab can usually turn E-6 process slides around in about three hours, and some claim as little as an hour-and-a-half. If you're in a hurry for your slides, or if you want a quick result on a test roll so that you can be sure your setup is working before you proceed with the bulk of your photography, this is the way to go. And a professional lab's experienced personnel are usually available for advice, should you have questions about your results.

## EVALUATING YOUR RESULTS

Don't despair if, in spite of your best efforts, the first film you get back from the photo lab or photo finisher is disappointing. While the techniques and equipment described herein should give you excellent results, a lot of variables are involved, and even professionals sometimes shoot preliminary tests for color and exposure, so that they can make adjustments and corrections if necessary.

If possible, evaluate your results on a photo lab's lightbox. This special box has a color temperature of 5000 degrees Kelvin, corresponding to daylight, which is the industry's viewing standard. In fact, many galleries will evaluate your artwork by scrutinizing your slides with a magnifying "loup" on a lightbox, rather than projecting them. If you have access to a projector, by all means look at your slides with it; it's a more critical test, and can reveal a lack of sharpness that's not apparent when the slide is viewed on a lightbox. But in terms of color, a slide that looks fine in the yellowish tungsten light of a projector may appear somewhat blue in color on a lightbox, so use the box as a color and exposure standard whenever possible. Never evaluate your slides by holding them up to the light of a window, or to a bright, exposed lightbulb. Even severely underexposed slides may appear fine with such a bright light source behind them.

In a pinch, a soft, translucent lampshade will do as a slide-viewing source, but because these will vary in brightness, be careful. You can even improvise a lightbox by propping a piece of glass on books or blocks of wood, or between tables, leaving plenty of room underneath for a clip-on light fixture. Use a relatively low-wattage bulb—60 or 75 watts— and place a sheet of heavy tracing paper over the glass to reduce and diffuse the light. If you have it, translucent Plexiglas can be used instead. When it comes time to mask your slides, you may have to resort to this. Keep in mind that tungsten light will make the slide appear warmer (i.e., yellower) in color than a light-box.

## JUDGING COLOR

Look critically at your slides. Does the color seem true to the original? A fairly neutral tone, such as a gray, or a pale or pastel color, is usually the best indication of the correctness of the slide's color. Slight variations in hue are harder to detect in more highly saturated colors. In fact, it's customary in photographs of artwork intended for reproduction to include the gray card that you've been using to determine exposure, butting it up against the side of a painting or print or placing it as unobtrusively as possible in a photograph of a three-dimensional work. Any color shift will be more easily detectable in the card's neutral gray than in the colors of the work itself, and its inclusion is particularly helpful to the lab technician making a color print from a negative. He or she can use it as a basis for determining color filtration, then crop it out to make the final print. If included in a slide, the card can be masked out with special tape, but in many circumstances it may be intrusive, and if the slide is intended for submission to a gallery or other promotional uses, you may prefer to leave it out, and evaluate color on the basis of your knowledge of the work.

The best way to assess the slide side-by-side with the artwork is to view it by the same kind of light that illuminates the work itself. If you've got tungsten light on the piece, for example, bounce the same light off a neutral white card to view the slide.

## COLOR VARIATIONS

Color variations are likely to occur along two lines: one, from yellow to blue, and two, from magenta to green. (Yellow and blue are complementary colors in light, as are magenta and green; these relationships form the basis for corrective filtration on the camera.)

**Slide Too Blue with Tungsten Film.** If your slide is too blue, and you're shooting an individual piece in controlled tungsten light with tungsten film, the most obvious culprit is stray daylight. If you think this is the problem, simply baffle out the daylight more carefully, or shoot at night. But there may be other causes for a blue cast. One is that you are using bulbs rated for 3400 degrees Kelvin, such as the DXCs recommended in chapter 2, with a film balanced for 3200 degree light. The most economical solution in this case is to shoot Kodachrome KPA, which is balanced for 3400 degree light. A more expensive alternative would be to replace the bulbs with lamps rated for 3200 degree light, such as the EALs recommended in chapter 2.

Even with 3200 degree color-rated bulbs, however, tungsten Ektachrome film may display a tendency to a blue cast, most evident in light tones. (This is also true of daylight-balanced Ektachrome in daylight.) The use of a warming filter, such as an 81 or 81A, will take this blue edge off the slide. If your work is very delicate or pale, it's a good idea to use such a filter from the start. If you're shooting three-dimensional work, you may notice that a white seamless tends to go blue as it recedes from your light source and becomes darker. A warming filter may minimize this, but to eliminate it entirely you may have to throw more light on the background. Dark grounds are less prone to this effect.

**Slide Too Blue with Daylight Film.** If your slide is too blue and you're shooting exhibition views or work installed outdoors with daylight film, blue skylight is usually the cause. Again, Ektachrome films display this tendency more than the Kodachromes, but even the E-6 process daylight films made by other manufacturers may be less susceptible to it. Short of switching to another film, though, corrective filtration may be used on the camera. While an 81A or 81B filter will produce an obvious warming effect, even the clear ultraviolet (UV) or skylight filter that many photographers use for lens protection will eliminate some blueness. Any of these filters will also help correct the bluish cast that shooting on an overcast day may produce. Finally, time of day can affect the color rendition of daylight film; if your results seem blue, you can try shooting at the end of the day, when the sun's long rays are warmed by atmospheric diffusion.

If you're using daylight film indoors, then you're probably shooting an exhibition of your work in a space that's predominantly or significantly window-lighted. If your result is too blue in these circumstances, you're more limited in what adjustments you can make, particularly if your work is also illuminated by tungsten gallery lights. Often the daylit areas of the space will be rendered too blue, and the artificially lighted areas too yellow because of the way daylight film "sees" tungsten light. Using a warming filter to correct the blue area will render the artwork even yellower than it is already, so use this procedure only if you can toler-

ate the extra warmth.

If your primary light source is daylight, and your slide is exceedingly blue, one final possibility is that you accidentally used tungsten-balanced film. As described on page 23, a tungsten-balanced film "sees" daylight as extremely blue in color. If you must use tungsten film in daylight, an 85B filter will correct this cast, but it's a much better idea to match your film balance with your light source.

**Slide Too Yellow.** If your slide is too yellow, there are several possible explanations. If the cast is strongly yellow-brown, almost golden, you may have used a daylight-balanced film in tungsten light. If you must shoot daylight film in tungsten light, an 80A or 80B filter will correct this cast, but it's a much better idea to switch to a tungsten-balanced film.

If you know you shot tungsten-balanced film, and the yellowish color is only slight, you may have photographed your work by regular tungsten illumination, rather than the light from the color-rated bulbs described in chapter 2. Buying color-rated bulbs will solve this problem. But if you're shooting installation views, or individual pieces by existing tungsten gallery light, you can't change all the bulbs, so if the cast is objectionable, you will have to use a cooling filter on the camera, such as an 82 or 82A.

Another possible cause of a yellowish cast is the use of tungsten Kodachrome KPA with tungsten bulbs other than the 3400 degree color-rated lamps it is meant to be used with, whether ordinary "household" tungsten or those color-rated for 3200 degrees Kelvin. Be sure to use DXC reflector photofloods or other 3400 degree bulbs with tungsten Kodachrome.

**Slide Too Green or Magenta.** The other "axis" along which color variations may occur is the green-magenta. Although less frequent, color shifts of this variety are often due to processing problems. If you're using a professional lab, check with them to see if they've been experiencing any problems with their E-6 line. If they won't confess to any, consider the following possibilities; if none of them is a factor, shoot another roll and see if the color cast appears again.

Fluorescent light will definitely cause a greenish cast in your photographs if it contributes any significant part of the light in them. Turn fluorescents off if possible, but if you can't, use corrective filtration on the camera such as that described in the section on filters. Eliminate any other light source, or else the portion of the lighting it contributes will be colored by the filter.

Similar filtration can be used to correct the greenish cast that certain daylight films may acquire at slow shutter speeds. But it's better to avoid such speeds, following the manufacturer's recommendation on the range of shutter speeds the film is designed for.

A magenta or reddish cast is more difficult to pinpoint. Both daylight and tungsten versions of Kodachrome are inclined to pick up a pinkish tint, for reasons not always easy to establish. But often such slight variations in color are attributable to shutter speeds outside the range suggested for the film. High-speed Ektachrome, for example, tends to turn cyan—the photographic term for blue-green—at shutter speeds slower than half a second, as does daylight Kodachrome (ISO 64). And at exposure times approaching ten seconds, tungsten Kodachrome tends to turn blue. Daylight Ektachrome, on the other hand, tends to turn yellow.

## OTHER COLOR FACTORS

Another factor in the color of a slide may be the color of the room you took it in. If the room is small, some of the light illuminating the artwork may have been bounced off its walls, ceiling, and floor, and if any of these surfaces has a strong color, it can color the slide. Even light bouncing off a shiny wooden floor can contribute its warmth to the artwork. If you suspect the room, move to another of more neutral color, or cover the offending surfaces with white sheets. Remember that if you want to use a room's walls or ceiling as bounce-light surfaces in shooting three-dimensional work, they must be of neutral tone, preferably white, or else they will contribute a color cast to the slide.

There may be times when you can't diagnose a chronic color problem, and in these cases it may be easier to use corrective filters on the camera. While some of the appropriate filters may be available in glass-mounted, screw-in form, others will only be available in optical gelatins. See the section on filters for more information.

## OTHER PROBLEMS

Color problems are more difficult to diagnose than any of the other complaints you may have about your finished slide. And solutions to problems not having to do with color fidelity are usually more self-evident. Lack of squareness in a flat artwork, for example, can be avoided in your next attempt by more careful squaring up. Refresh your memory as to the proper procedure by reviewing the box on page 43, and be more patient next time.

If in the finished slide an artwork is shifted from its observed posi-tion in the camera's viewfinder, you will have to get into the habit of placing it off-center in the other direction when framing or squaring it up, so that it will end up in the proper place. The degree, if any, to which the image is shifted in this way varies greatly from one camera to the next.

## LACK OF SHARPNESS

Lack of sharpness in a slide or print can have a number of causes. One of the most common, yet most frequently ignored, is a dirty or smudged lens or filter. While a small sprinkling of dust will have a negligible effect on the image, a greasy fingerprint can make the sharpest lens render your artwork with a romantic fog. Grime can build up slowly, too. Refer to the box on page 18, chapter 1, for an explanation of how to clean a lens, and check yours frequently for cleanliness.

If your lens is clean but your slide is still unsharp, you may have focused incorrectly. At the smaller lens apertures that are advisable in photographing artwork, your depth of field should be adequate to compensate for small errors in focus. Improper focus is a likely suspect in an unsharp image if some parts of your subject seem clearer than others. In a three-dimensional artwork, for example, if the closest part of the piece is sharp but none of the rest is, you focused in front of the piece, rather than a third of the way into it, as suggested earlier. If the background in an installation view is sharp, but the foreground fuzzy, you didn't focus close enough.

**Bad Vibes.** An overall lack of sharpness is often due to camera movement. If you hand-held the camera, your own unsteadiness is probably at fault. If you insist on holding the camera, you may need to use a faster shutter speed to avoid the problem, although this will force you to use wider apertures to obtain proper exposure, thus reducing your depth of field. It's better to use a tripod, so that you can use slower shutter speeds, and rule yourself out as a variable.

Even if you use a tripod, there are a couple of ways that vibrations can reduce the sharpness of your slide. One is manual triggering of the shutter, that is, with your finger on the button, rather than with a cable release. Any hand pressure will shake the camera at the slow shutter speeds necessary in photographing artwork by tungsten light. If you've lost or forgotten the cable release, use the camera's self-timer to trigger the shutter, setting it at its longest interval so that any vibrations have time to subside.

Vibrations may also occur when you advance the film to expose successive frames. It's important to wait at least ten seconds after advancing the film before you trip the shutter again, to give the vibrations a chance to dissipate.

Other less likely causes of lack of sharpness have to do with the lens itself. If it's been abused, its internal elements may have loosened, making it impossible for the lens to resolve an image clearly. The only solution to this problem is a costly repair, or replacement of the lens. Also, some lenses tend to produce less sharp images at very small or very wide apertures. This has to do with certain optical properties of the lens, not with depth of field. You're unlikely to be shooting at these apertures, however.

## EXPOSURE PROBLEMS

Exposure problems—that is, a result that is too dark or too light—are unlikely if you observe the recommendations made in these pages, and if you are careful to bracket your exposures. But sometimes they can be caused by a bad light meter, an inaccurate shutter, or, less often, a sticky lens aperture or malfunctioning coupling. A lens with an aperture or aperture-coupling problem *must* be fixed, but if the culprit is your shutter or meter, you can attempt to determine just how far off the result is, and adjust for that difference when you calculate the proper exposure. If the result seems a stop darker—that is, less exposed—than it should be, you should add a stop to the exposure indicated by your gray card reading, either by using a slower shutter speed or a wider aperture. If you're using an automatic camera, set the exposure compensation dial to +1. If your result seems a half-stop lighter—more exposed—than it should be, then decrease your indicated exposure by a half-stop, either manually or by setting an automatic camera's exposure compensation dial to -½.

The problem with making these adjustments consistently is that a meter may be more or less accurate at certain light levels, and a shutter more or less accurate at certain speeds. If you suspect a mechanical or electronic problem, you're better off getting it fixed than trying to predict its behavior.

As always, be sure to bracket your exposures, however you adjust them, and bracket them heavily if you're nervous about the result. Better to waste a little film than have to repeat the entire operation.

## SUMMARY/ **EVALUATING YOUR RESULTS**

- Have your film processed by a reputable professional lab or photo finisher.
- Have black and white film processed by a professional lab specializing in black and white, if possible.
- The turnaround time on slide film processing is often short enough so that you can leave your setup intact and reshoot if necessary.
- When possible, use a color-rated lightbox to evaluate your slides. Don't hold them up to a window to judge exposure and color; the person you're sending them to probably won't.
- If you shoot tungsten film and your slide comes back too blue, it's due either to the presence of daylight, to using 3400-degree bulbs with 3200-degree-balanced film, or to the general tendency of Ektachrome to run blue. Eliminate extraneous light sources, use compatible bulbs and film and/or put a warming filter on your lens. (If your result is extremely blue, you may have used tungsten film in daylight.)
- If you shoot daylight film and your slide comes back too blue, the problem is usually due to the presence of blue skylight, as in indirect window light or open shade. Use a warming filter if you must shoot in the same light again.
- If your slide is too yellow, you either shot daylight film in tungsten light, or tungsten film in light of lower color temperature than the film is balanced for. If the problem can't be corrected by matching light and film more closely, consider blue filtration on the camera.
- If your slide is too green, it's often due to the presence of fluorescent light. (Fluorescent light will produce a bluish-green cast on tungsten film.) Use a CC 30 Magenta filter with daylight film if you must shoot under fluorescent light, and eliminate all other light sources.
- Shifts toward magenta or green are on occasion due to film processing problems. To determine this, shoot another roll to see if the problem disappears.
- The color of the room you're shooting in can contribute a color cast to the work, particularly if the room is small and brightly colored.
- Color filters may be used on the camera to correct a chronic color problem. Consult your local lab if you're unable to determine which to use.
- Lack of sharpness can be caused by a dirty or smudged lens or filter; improper focus and/or inadequate depth of field; camera movement.
- Incorrect exposure can be caused by improper light-metering technique and mechanical problems in the camera. If your slides are always underexposed, increase your exposure; if they are overexposed, reduce it. Always be sure to bracket your exposures, which may make up for such problems.

## PHOTOGRAPHING SMALL ARTWORK

The "normal" 50mm lens on your camera probably doesn't focus much closer than two or three feet. And with most telephoto and many zoom lenses, you must be even further away from a subject to focus it sharply. This limited close-focusing distance may make it impossible to make small artworks such as jewelry (even small prints) fill the view finder frame, and thus the finished slide. Some photography labs can make a custom duplicate slide in which a portion of your original slide—your artwork—is enlarged to fill the frame, and in a print the image can always be enlarged and cropped to size. (If you're having a commercial print made, ask for a larger size and trim it down.) But any time you enlarge and/or duplicate your original image, you compromise its quality, so it's better to make your original as much to your liking as possible. With small artwork, this may require the use of additional equipment, some of it moderate in price, some of it more expensive.

**"Macro" Zooms.** The solution, however, may be as easy as throwing a switch on your lens barrel. Many of the zoom lenses that enjoy such popularity today offer a "macro," or close-focusing mode. If you have a zoom lens that offers this option, consult your lens manual to find out how to select it. The macro mode on some zooms allows you to get as close as five or six inches, depending on what focal length is set. If you have the choice, pick a focal length that is reasonable and suited to your artwork. Try to avoid settings shorter than 50mm and longer than 135mm, but some lenses may offer a limited choice of settings in macro mode. Focal length settings somewhat longer than the standard 50mm may minimize distortion in small three-dimensional work, and may be more practical in the extra room for lighting paraphernalia and arrangements they afford. But keep in mind that longer lenses offer less depth of field at a given aperture and focused distance, and depth of field is already shallow at such close distances.

**Macro Lenses.** By contrast, the most expensive solution to the problem of shooting small artwork is to buy a macro lens, a lens of fixed focal length that will often focus close enough to produce a life-size image of a subject on film. The most commonly used focal length in a macro lens is 50- or 55mm, although these lenses are available in longer lengths such as 105mm. The latter may be more practical for very small artwork, because of the additional distance they put between the piece and you, but the standard 55mm focal length macro may be a better choice because it can double as a normal lens. (Macro lenses will focus from their closest focusing distance all the way to infinity.) In fact, if you're in the market for a new camera, and you do small artwork that you plan to photograph regularly, you might want to substitute a 55mm macro lens for the standard 50mm lens that is usually supplied with the camera. This will entail an additional cost, because macro lenses are more expensive than lenses of conventional design, but the lens' convenience and ease of use may be worth the price. Like regular lenses, a macro is fully coupled to the camera, preserving all its normal functions.

**Close-Up Lenses.** A far less expensive alternative to the macro lens, and one that also allows the camera's metering and lens-linkage systems to function normally, is the use of add-on close-up lenses. Close-up lenses usually come in sets of three, and screw into the front thread of your camera's lens just like filters. (They're sized like filters, too.) Each one corrects your 50mm lens so that it is able to resolve subjects in specific close-up ranges. Combining them will give the lens even higher close-focusing power, but may reduce the sharpness of your image slightly. Check the close-up lens instructions, or experiment to see which lens or combination of lenses is best for your work's particular size.

**Other Close-Up Equipment.** Finally, you can increase the close-focusing capability of any lens by placing one or more *extension tubes* between it and the camera body. These fittings must obviously be designed to accommodate the particular lens-mounting system of your camera. The more expensive of them preserve camera-to-lens functions, but are considerably more costly than add-on close-up lenses, although they pose no threat to the sharpness of the image. The less expensive ones are closer in price to close-up lenses, but because they interrupt the automatic camera-to-lens linkage, you have to take your light readings before inserting them, and increase the exposure (the instructions that come with the tubes tell how) to compensate for the additional distance the light from the lens must travel.

Because nonautomatic tubes prevent the camera from keeping

the lens diaphragm open during viewing, you will have to set the lens to its widest aperture to frame up your work, then stop it down manually to the correct shooting aperture before taking your picture. (This will cause the viewfinder to darken considerably if you're using a small aperture.)

A similar option involves an actual bellows with hardware at either end that may or may not permit automatic operation of the lens. But these units are more suited to the photography of very small objects, and can cost as much as a lens. Unless your work is literally postage-stamp size, you're better off purchasing a macro lens, the close-focusing range of which can be extended even further with the use of the attachments described previously.

**Choice of Aperture.** One of the most important things to remember in shooting small artwork (especially if it's three-dimensional) is that you must use smaller apertures than larger artwork would require. This is because at close focused distances, any lens' depth of field is more limited. Stopping the lens down to an aperture of f16, or, if your camera offers it, even f22 (a macro lens usually stops down to f32), may require the use of slower shutter speeds, but you can make up for this in part by moving your lights closer to the work for additional brightness. This is an option because smaller work can be lighted evenly from closer distances. Be careful, as always, not to put delicate artwork at risk from the heat that the lamps generate.

**Focusing Close-Up Subjects.** Because depth of field is shallow at such close distances, proper focusing becomes much more critical. A one-inch error in focusing a large work will be more than compensated for by the depth of field provided

by moderate lens apertures (f8, f11), but in a small work, it may mean the difference between sharpness and fuzziness.

Unless your work is free standing, you may want to consider the use of a copy stand, described in the chapter on two-dimensional work. The copy stand is also quite useful for small three-dimensional work that you want to shoot down on like jewelry or bowls. Using a tripod to do this may present problems, particularly if you have to overextend its legs, making it unsteady.

## FILTERS

If the color temperature of your light source matches the color balance of the film you're using, in theory the colors in your slide should be true to your artwork. In practice, this isn't always the case. If you're convinced you're observing every precaution, and the color of your slides is still off, then you may find it easier to use filters over the lens to adjust the color.

### HOW FILTERS WORK

Any colored filter works by blocking varying degrees of light complementary in color to the filter. (Color relationships in light are somewhat different than those in pigment. Red and green make yellow in light, mud in paint.) A yellow filter, for example, will reduce the amount of blue light reaching the film, thereby producing a yellower color slide. This is how the 81-series filters described in the box on page 25 work. In a black and white image, a yellow filter will make any blue object's tone darker relative to other values. A magenta-colored filter will, for the same reason, reduce the amount of green light reaching the film, which is why it is recommended for shooting in fluorescent light, which produces a greenish cast on day-

light film. The amount of light a colored filter blocks is proportional to the strength of its color.

### KINDS OF FILTERS

There are basically two types of filters for color film, although they overlap and can be interchanged to some extent. One is the color conversion or light-balancing series, designated by a number in the eighties, and usually a letter from A to EF. The color of these filters is based on differences in the color temperature of light, as discussed in chapter 2. The 81 and 85 series filters are yellowish or yellowish-orange in color; the 80 and 82 series are bluish. The 85 series filters have stronger color, and a more pronounced effect on color film, than the 81 series, and the 80 series has a stronger effect than the 82 series. Use of an orangy 85B filter, for example, will allow you to shoot tungsten film outdoors, because it makes daylight "look" like tungsten light to the film. A strong blue 80A filter will do just the opposite: produce more or less correct color when shooting daylight film in tungsten light. This filter is useful when you want to shoot color negative film, which is balanced for daylight, in 3200 degree tungsten light.

**A Delicate Balance.** The 81 and 82 series light-balancing filters are more useful. As mentioned, an 81 series filter will give varying degrees of warmth to a slide, starting with the very slight effect of an 81, to the strong warming of an 81C or 81EF. If your slides have a bluish cast, these filters will eliminate it if all other factors are the same the next time you photograph your work. Their effect, and for the most part the effect of any colored filter, can be observed by placing them over the offending slide on a lightbox, as described in the last chapter. If your slide has a yellow cast that you'd like to avoid next time, an 82 series filter will usually take care of it. The warm result that low-intensity tungsten light will produce on tungsten film can be minimized or eliminated, for example, by using an 82A or an 82B filter over the lens. As with the 81 series filters, the effect of these filters is stronger with each successive letter. (See pages 112-113.)

**Color Compensation.** The other option in color filtration is the color-compensating filter, designated with a "CC." These filters come in three sets of complementary colors: yellow and blue, magenta and green, and cyan (blue-green) and red. Each color is available in a wide range of strengths, indicated by numbers, and will reduce the presence of its complement in a slide according to the size of its number. A CC 30 Magenta is more intense, for example, than a CC 05 Magenta, which is why it corrects the strong greenish cast caused by fluorescent light.

Filters of a given CC number have equal strength—a CC 30 Red will cancel out a CC 30 Cyan, producing a neutral gray density. You can combine filters to achieve a certain level of correction. A CC 20 Blue with a CC 05 Blue equals CC 25 Blue, while a CC 20 Blue with a CC 05 Yellow (the complement of blue) equals CC 15 Blue. The latter could also be achieved by combining a CC 10 Blue and a CC 05 Blue, of course.

Use of CC filters is, as with all color filtration, a somewhat subjective thing. A slide that someone else considers too yellow may look fine to you. But if you aren't happy with the color of your results, and you plan to shoot again in the same situation, you may elect to use a filter. Go to a professional lab if you want help determining the needed correction. A chart for achieving color balance under fluorescent lighting is on page 100.

### OTHER FILTERS

If you're shooting outdoors, consider using a clear glass UV or skylight filter to eliminate the ultraviolet component of daylight that your film records, but that your eye doesn't see. Depending on conditions, ultraviolet light can make a photograph of something look bluer or hazier than it actually is. Many photographers keep one of these filters over the lens at all times to protect it, but if you're using other filters, it should be taken off to avoid degradation of the image. Numbers 2A and 2B filters will cut out even more UV light, but may make the image appear overly warm. (The 2A is the stronger of the two.) Ultraviolet filters are almost colorless, and their effect on a subject can't be observed on a lightbox.

In shooting black and white film outdoors in sunny conditions, a medium yellow filter over the lens will produce a more normal-looking sky in the print, improving cloud definition by deepening the surrounding blue areas. This filter is specifically designed for black and white work, and goes by the designation "Y," "K2," or "Wratten #8" (a Kodak gelatin), depending on the brand.

**Polarizing Filter.** A polarizing filter does much the same thing with color film outdoors, but it is more useful as a means of controlling or eliminating unwanted reflections in a subject. A variation on Polaroid sunglasses, the filter, which is neutral gray in color, can minimize the glare that occurs on the edges of even the most carefully lighted high-gloss or heavily textured paintings. (It is also useful in reducing glare on cracks and crazing in older paintings.) The filter will not, however, eliminate a direct reflection; the angle at which the light glances off the surface must be fairly oblique. And because the filter is actually a microscopic grid, it must be oriented in a certain way relative to the light source in order to work. For this reason, it's designed to allow for rotation in its mount, the effect of which can be observed through the camera. Turn it until glare is at a minimum. (Needless to say, the effect of this filter can't be observed on a lightbox either.)

The polarizing filter is even more effective if used in combination with polarized light sources. You can polarize your lights by placing a sheet of polarizing film in front of your lamps, being sure all light falling on the subject area passes through the sheet, but keeping the sheet far enough away from the lamp to avoid melting or burning it. Reflections can be virtually eliminated if you turn the filter so that it's perpendicular to the angle at which the lights are polarized. The effect can be observed in the camera's viewfinder as you turn the filter, but you will notice an overall darkening of the image as well as a change in the reflection. This technique, called *cross-polarization*, may be useful in eliminating the reflection of your light source on shiny non-metallic three-dimensional pieces, such as high-glaze ceramics. But it reduces the light reaching your film dramatically, requiring a three- or four-stop increase in exposure time and/or lens aperture size to obtain correct exposure. (More light or higher-speed film will counteract this to some extent.) It may also turn specular highlights (the actual reflection of the light source) a violet color, and will increase the contrast of your slide considerably. Both single- and cross-polarization will increase, perhaps even distort

# SHOOTING IN FLUORESCENT LIGHT
## COLOR BALANCE AND FILTRATION

The most frequently used fluorescent lamp is the cool white type, which will yield reasonably neutral color on daylight film if a CC 30 Magenta filter is used on the camera, as described in the text. The chart below tells you the film to use and the proper color filtration for other kinds of fluorescent light. If only one film type is given, it is because it is much closer in terms of color balance to the lamp's light, and thus requires the least amount of corrective filtration. (Any film type can be made to record correct color in fluorescent light with the right filtration: consult Kodak's *Professional Photoguide* for this information.)

| Fluorescent Lamp Type | Film Type and Color Filtration |
|---|---|
| Cool White | Use daylight film with CC 30 Magenta filter |
| Cool White Deluxe | Use Type A film (Kodachrome KPA) with CC 10 Red + CC 10 Yellow filters or Type B film (tungsten Ektachrome) with CC 10 Red + CC 20 Yellow filters |
| Warm White | Use Type A film (Kodachrome KPA) with CC 20 Magenta + CC 10 Red filters or Type B film (tungsten Ektachrome) with CC 10 Magenta + CC 20 Red filters |
| Warm White Deluxe | Use Type A film (Kodachrome KPA) without filter or Type B film (tungsten Ektachrome) with CC 10 Yellow filter |
| White | Use Type B film (tungsten Ektachrome) with CC 40 Red filter |
| Daylight | Use daylight film with CC 30 Red + CC 10 Magenta filters |

the intensity of colors in your work, because they screen out the "scattered" light that tends to wash out colors, and which is a component of the light we perceive in looking at an artwork.

## EXPOSURE CORRECTION WITH FILTERS

Any filter will reduce the amount of light reaching the film. With filters of moderate density or color, such as the 81 or 82 series, or the lower numbers of color-correcting fil-

ters, this reduction is very slight. With a color conversion filter such as an 80A, however, it is as much as two or more stops, a reduction that may force you to use overly wide f-stops or slow shutter speeds that may cause reciprocity failure or color shifts. In such cases, you may want to consider the use of higher-speed films or extra light to compensate.

Your camera's through-the-lens meter will compensate reasonably well for the addition of a filter of moderate effect (and/or neutral color, such as the polarizing filter), indicating the need for slight adjustments in aperture or shutter speed. But with filters of strong color, the filter's effect on the colors of your artwork—particularly if a single color predominates in it—may begin to throw off your camera's meter. In this case, it's advisable to bracket your exposures even more heavily than you ordinarily would. If you want to be sure the increase in exposure that your camera recommends or makes is correct, check the *filter factor* of the filter you want to use. In a glass filter, it will usually be indicated in the literature supplied with the filter. A filter factor of 2, for example, means that exposure must be increased by a stop (i.e., doubled) if the filter is used; if it's 3, by a stop and a half; if it's 4, by two stops. In fact, you have the option of taking your gray card readings without the filter in place, then increasing the indicated exposure by the factor recommended for the filter.

## GLASS VS. GELATIN

Most commonly used filters are available in glass-mounted, screw-in types, an advantage of which is that they are relatively scratch-resistant and can be easily cleaned should they become smudged or dirty. Be sure you buy them in a size that fits the front thread of your lens, the diameter of which is usually indicated in millimeters on the end of its barrel, next to a special symbol.

If you can't get a specific filter in glass, you may have to buy it in an optical gelatin manufactured by Kodak. The most useful and common size is a three-inch square. Gelatin filters cost as much as glass filters, but are more delicate. Because they can't be cleaned, you should treat them with extra care, returning them to their package when you've finished using them. Because gelatin filters aren't rigid, you'll have to improvise a cardboard frame for them, or purchase either a clip-on filter holder or a metal filter frame. A cardboard or metal frame will then have to be taped to the lens. Store filters in a cool, dry place. Some purists argue that gelatin filters are optically better than glass, allowing you to use as many as three sandwiched together, a bad idea with glass filters, but few of us will notice the difference. The only real advantage to them is that virtually every kind of filter is available in gelatin. Some manufacturers produce sturdier, square plastic laminate filters in a range almost as broad as the Kodak gelatin filters; these can be cleaned and even polished to eliminate scratches, but can be twice as expensive as gelatin filters.

Which brings us to the bottom line: cost. Glass filters vary quite a bit in price, depending on their size, type, and manufacturer. Some camera makers' proprietary filters may cost fifteen to twenty dollars, but there is often little difference in optical quality between them and those made by companies that specialize in camera accessories. Filters from these companies cost under ten dollars, and as little as six or seven dollars at a

good discount. A polarizing filter is usually twice as expensive as a colored glass filter, because of its special design. Kodak's gelatin filters cost as much as colored glass filters (nine dollars or more), a high price given their fragility. Try to buy filters in glass whenever possible.

## DUPLICATING SLIDES

It's hard to predict just what the demand for slides of your work will be, and there may be times when you have to have duplicates made. Although a dupe is never as high in quality as a good original slide, a reputable professional lab will have its duplicating process down to a science that brings it pretty close. One of the drawbacks to duping a slide is that it can increase the contrast of the original, making a slide with subtle hues and tonalities look somewhat garish. If the original is rather flat-looking, on the other hand, duping it can give it the extra snap it needs. (Pushing film, described later in this chapter, is a way of increasing the contrast of an *original* slide.)

If you have a choice of lighter and darker exposure brackets, dupe the darker one, provided it's of acceptable exposure. This is particularly important if the slide has light highlights, because the increase in contrast in the dupe can cause them to be washed out. Keep in mind, too, that duplicating a slide necessarily crops a small part of the outside of the image area. For this reason, if you're making a slide specifically for duping, you may want to leave a little more margin than you ordinarily would.

### CUSTOM DUPING

Duping can also be a way of correcting problems in an original slide, although you will have to pay the lab "custom" prices—usually

two or three times the cost of a regular dupe—for this service. If your slide has an unwanted color cast, the lab can make a duplicate in which a filter is used to compensate for it. (See page 99.) A bluish cast can be corrected with yellow filtration, for example.

A duplicate slide can also be made in which a portion of your original is enlarged to full-frame 35mm size. This service may be useful if, for some reason, you weren't able to get close enough to your artwork to make it fill the frame, such as in shooting small artwork with a 50mm lens and no close-up attachments. But excessive enlargements of this sort should be avoided, because they compromise the quality of the original.

A custom lab can also make an *enlarged* duplicate transparency for you, blowing your 35mm slide up to 4x5-inch or even 8x10-inch size. You will pay prices many times higher than those for 35mm-size duplicates for this service, but it may make for a more impressive presentation in cases when larger formats are acceptable. An enlarged duplicate is never a substitute for a good large-format transparency, the quality of which it can never approach. For reproduction purposes, you're better off using an original slide than an enlarged duplicate.

## MASKING SLIDES

The two-to-three ratio of the 35mm format—a rather long rectangle—is often unsuited to the proportions of your artwork. If your work is two-dimensional, the closer it is to a square, the more empty area there will be on either side of it in the finished slide. This can also be a problem with three-dimensional work, although if the background material fills the

Masking slides.

frame, it may still look present-able. Black paper behind a two-dimensional work will eliminate any extraneous details, and give the artwork more brilliance in the contrast it provides. (With a dark work it may be better to substitute white paper or a white sheet.) If projected, however, even the blackest background will transmit some light, showing the surface texture of the material.

You can prevent this by masking these areas out with a thin, opaque tape made especially for use on slides. Leitz produces it in a shiny silver version, Kodak in a black, somewhat thicker one. Buy it in as narrow a roll as possible.

### RIGHT SIDE UP
When you mask a slide, you must always place the tape on the *base* side of the film, never the *emulsion* side. If you try to reposition tape placed on the emulsion side of the film, you may tear the image off. The base side of the film is the side that faces you when your subject is correctly oriented (not backwards)

in the mount. It is also completely smooth, in contrast to the emulsion side, which looks bumpy when you hold it at an angle to the light.

To mask the slide, cut a piece of tape quite a bit longer than the short side of the slide's image area, which is probably the side you'll be masking. This will give you a "handle" to grip when positioning it. If you have to cut the tape lengthwise to make a narrower strip, always orient the precut side (from the outside of the roll) toward the artwork, so that the edge will be perfectly straight. Place the tape against the slide, letting it run over the mount on the long side of the image area, and keeping it parallel either with the edge of a two-dimensional work, or in the case of a three-dimensional work, with the inside edge of the slide mount. If the tape's cockeyed, pull it up and reposition it. If you'd rather, you can put a second piece over it to correct the edge. (This will also eliminate occasional pinholes in the tape.) In some instances, you may

have to overlap the tape to make it cover the area you want to mask.

Cut off any excess tape, letting it extend onto the slide mount from the image area. Don't trim it at the inside edge of the mount. Keep the roll of tape in a plastic bag; if you don't, the edges will pick up lint and dust, which if projected will be magnified many times.

Don't mask slides before duping them. Although a professional lab may be able to produce a good dupe from a masked slide because each original is assessed by hand, a commercial photo finisher's automated averaging system may try to adjust the dupe for what it sees as an extremely dark original slide. The result may be an overexposed dupe.

## CLEANING SLIDES
If you want to dupe an original slide that's seen a few fingers in its day, you should clean it carefully beforehand. Commercial film cleaning solvents are available in small bottles; be sure you get one that's designed for color film. Apply it with a surgical-quality cotton ball; wet each side of the slide with a circular motion, then buff the slide lightly with a dry cotton ball.

## SHOOTING NEGATIVE FILM
Nine times out of ten you will be making slides of your work. On some occasions you will need prints, though, and this may require the use of different films than those discussed earlier in the book. "Print" films, as they are sometimes called, reverse the tones and colors of the subject, and from the resulting *negative* any number of positive prints can be made. A slide, by contrast, is the film that you actually ran through the camera.

A high-quality color print can

easily be made from a slide, and if you're shooting by tungsten light, this is probably the best route to take. Commercial photo finishers usually make a print from a slide with a throw-away internegative. A professional lab can also make a print from an internegative of your slide (this is sometimes called a *C-print*), but alternatively can make a *reversal print* directly from your slide. The lab will charge you extra for the internegative, making a C-print doubly expensive, but both kinds of prints cost considerably more than a photo finisher's color print. Ordinarily, though, the quality of a lab's print is better because it's made by a human being instead of a machine.

## PRINT GRADES

Professional labs usually offer several grades of print, whether color or black and white. The least expensive buys you a limited amount of darkroom manipulation, should it be needed, but tricky or poor-quality negatives (or slides) may require extra work. This costs more, so it behooves you to be meticulous in your lighting and film exposure technique. The extra money also usually gets you a print over which you have final approval; within reason, the lab will reprint it as many times as necessary to make it to your liking.

There are limits to what a color or black and white printer can do, however, and at best, printing is a somewhat interpretive science. Color can be added or subtracted at will, and exposure can be varied to make the image lighter or darker. Because the printer has never seen your work, he may print it wrong. This is a particular risk for a color negative, which bears little resemblance to its subject. A slide, on the other hand, is its own positive standard; the printer simply needs to make the print match it as

closely as possible. In fact, if you're having a print made from a color negative (even a black and white negative), it's not a bad idea to leave an accurate slide of your work with the lab.

**Gray Card.** If you're planning to make a slide or negative specifically for printing and/or for reproduction, it's also a good idea to leave the gray card you've been using for light readings *in* the photograph, if this can be done discreetly. With a two-dimensional work, simply butt the card up against the edge of the piece. With a three-dimensional work, prop it up along the edges of the frame so that it can be cropped out in the print. Even a narrow strip of the card can be useful to the printer; its neutral gray gives him a known value and color standard on which to base his exposure and color filtration. Mention to the lab's clerk that you've included the gray card in the photograph.

## BLACK AND WHITE FILM

Black and white film reduces the colors of your artwork to shades of gray, making a black and white print an imperfect record of your artwork at best. But you will, on occasion, have to supply black and white prints of your work, usually for publicity purposes and newspaper reproduction. Particularly in an inexpensive halftone reproduction, a good print can mean the difference between a reproduction that is pure mud and one that is crisp and clear.

Getting a good black and white print is easier said than done because of the generally poor quality of commercial black and white lab work. Professional color labs that do excellent color work will often wreak havoc with your black and white film, canceling out your sincere effort at photographing your artwork. Your best bet is to seek out a good photo lab that specializes in black and white work. As an alternative, consider having a photography student do the necessary darkroom work. If neither of these options is available, you may be better off sending your film to Kodak than entrusting it to a color lab.

**B&W and Light.** One advantage to shooting in black and white is that for all practical purposes, the film doesn't "see" the differences in the color of light that can create such problems when shooting in color. You can use tungsten light, daylight, or a combination of the two, although the tungsten lamps recommended in chapter 2 permit greater control in shooting individual works. But in a pinch, you can shoot by window light, in overcast, open shade, or any other kind of light, provided it's appropriate in quality to the subject, without corrective filtration.

As with color film, you should choose a black and white film with fine grain and good sharpness, so that your artwork will be clearly and smoothly rendered in the print. An ISO 125 film, such as Kodak's Plus-X Pan, is a practical choice, because it offers reasonable speed in addition to fine grain. It's not a bad idea to give it a little extra exposure by setting your camera's ISO dial to 100 or even lower, because commercial photo finishers, and even professional black and white labs, tend to give the film less than optimum development. Nonetheless, you should bracket your exposures just as you would when shooting color film, to give the printer a negative of the best possible density.

"Faster" black and white films, those with an ISO of 400, may be useful in photographing installation views in low light. Even in an $8 \times 10$-inch enlargement, these films display moderately fine grain. But if you're using a tripod, longer exposures should make the ISO 125 film perfectly practical even for this application.

## COLOR NEGATIVE FILM

All 35mm color negative films are balanced for daylight. Shooting them in tungsten light results in a negative that, if uncorrected, will produce a print with a strong brownish-yellow cast. The negative can be made to produce a normal-looking print through careful filtration in the enlarger, not very likely with a machine-made print. A custom lab may charge you a premium for a print requiring such an extreme correction. If you want to shoot color negative film, it's best to filter it on the camera with an 80A color conversion filter, which makes tungsten light "look" like the daylight the film wants to see.

Because this filter reduces the light reaching the film by two stops, you may want to use a relatively high-speed film. When filtered with an 80A filter, a film with an ISO of 400 will require exposure settings equal to those of an ISO 100 film. The camera's through-the-lens meter should indicate these settings when the filter is in place, so set the film speed dial to the recommended ISO 400 if you use such a film. If you're concerned that the colors in your work might throw off the meter reading, take a gray-card reading without the filter and increase the indicated exposure by two stops for filtered photographs. (Refer back to page 98 for an explanation of filters.) If you elect to use a color negative film with finer grain, such as an ISO 100 or 200 film (Kodak's Vericolor III, with an ISO of 160, is a good compromise), be prepared to use slower shutter speeds to make up for the light loss caused by the filter. As always, bracket your exposures to give the printer a good range of negatives to choose from.

Current color films yield finer grain if overexposed slightly, and an extra half-stop of exposure actually makes a color negative print better. Bracketing your exposures will produce such a negative if your starting exposure is more or less correct, but if you want to build this extra exposure into your ISO setting, reduce it by about 25 percent from the film's nominal ISO. For ISO 400 film, for example, you should set the film speed dial to ISO 320 (the nearest number on the dial); with an ISO 200 film, set it to ISO 160.

## "PUSHING" FILM

"Pushing" is the popular term for giving photographic film extra development to compensate for underexposing it. The argument usually advanced for this technique is that it lets you take pictures in light that otherwise might be too dim to obtain good exposure, or lets you use smaller apertures or higher shutter speeds in more acceptable light levels. You push film by setting a higher ISO number than that recommended for the film, so that the camera's meter thinks the film is more sensitive than it really is, and instructs you or the camera to give it less exposure than it would ordinarily need. If film exposed this way is developed normally, the result is a slide that's too dark, but if the film is given extended development, chemical action adjusts for the underexposure, although with certain trade-offs.

Pushing film *one stop* will allow you to use a one-stop faster shutter speed or a one-stop smaller lens aperture. Set your camera's film speed (ISO) dial to a number double that of the recommended ISO for the film; with tungsten Ektachrome EPY, for example, set the control to 100 instead of 50. This will allow you to use a one-

step higher shutter speed, which may be useful when you're concerned that the length of an exposure may cause reciprocity failure (see page 72). Alternatively, it will let you use a one-stop smaller aperture, which can be helpful in improving depth of field when shooting three-dimensional artwork. When you deliver the film, specify that it be pushed one stop. Keep in mind that it's very important to bracket your exposures when you intend to push your film.

One effect of pushing film that can be either an advantage or a drawback is the increase in image contrast that it causes. This effect can be used to produce a better slide of an artwork with very close values and low inherent contrast, as illustrated in the color plates on page 111. If a one-stop push produces too contrasty a result, try a one-half stop push. For a half-stop push, set your ISO dial to a number 50 percent higher than the film's recommended ISO (increase High-Speed tungsten Ektachrome's 160 to 250, for example) and ask that the film be pushed a half-stop. Most custom photo labs will push film to exact specifications, and in general you should patronize professional outfits for this service, confining the technique to E-6 process films like the Ektachromes and Fujichromes. Kodak will adjust development to your specifications (including development of Kodachrome), but for a rather steep additional charge. Note that pushing film will make an already contrasty subject—such as an installation view with spotty light—even more contrasty, reducing detail in either the highlights, the shadows, or both. Pushing film may also change the slide's color slightly.

# SUMMARY/**PROFESSIONAL TIPS**

- Since conventional lenses won't focus close enough to let small artwork fill the frame, use a zoom lens with a macro capability or a filter-like close-up lens that can be screwed into a conventional lens's front thread.
- Extension tubes and bellows units can be used between the lens and camera body to permit very close focusing with a conventional lens, but some may interfere with the automatic coupling between lens and camera.
- Depth of field is extremely shallow at close focusing distances, making correct focus even more important.
- Filters may be used on the camera to control or alter the color rendition of a slide by reducing the amount of light of complementary color reaching the film. The stronger its color, the more light of complementary color it blocks.
- A polarizing filter may be used to control some kinds of reflections and glare, and will darken a blue sky. Its effect can be controlled and observed in the viewfinder by rotating the filter in its mount.
- In most cases, your camera's through-the-lens metering system will adjust the exposure it recommends or sets to compensate for the light-reducing presence of a filter. Taking the light reading off a gray card will minimize any error.
- If you're shooting in tungsten light, it's better to have a print made from a tungsten-balanced slide than from a color negative, which is balanced for daylight.
- If you want to shoot color negative film in tungsten light, an 80A or 80B filter's deep blue color will make the light "look" like the daylight the film wants to see. The filter reduces the amount of light entering the camera, and must be compensated for by the use of longer shutter speeds, wider lens apertures, or brighter light.
- Leaving a gray card along the edge of an artwork you're shooting a color negative of will help the printer at a professional lab establish the correct color filtration and exposure for the print.
- Negative films will produce better prints (particularly when processed by commercial labs) if given a little more exposure than the gray card reading would indicate. You can build this extra exposure into your reading by setting a slightly lower ISO than that recommended for the film you are using.
- "Pushing" film means extending a film's development time in processing to adjust for deliberate underexposure of the film.
- To expose film for "push" processing, you set a higher ISO than that recommended for the film. Because the camera's meter thinks the film is more sensitive to light than it actually is, it will recommend or set smaller apertures and/or faster shutter speeds.
- Pushing film also increases the contrast of a slide or print, which may produce a crisper image of an artwork with close values.

## STAINED GLASS

Stained glass is among the most difficult kind of two-dimensional artwork to photograph because it must be evenly backlighted. Pieces that contain opalescent or hand-painted glass, such as this handsome nineteenth-century window by John LaFarge, above, benefit from additional frontlighting, which in this case shows off the work's intricate leading and wooden frame.

## TOP LIGHT AND THREE-DIMENSIONAL WORK

Top light is often an effective alternative to side light, and some artworks are better served by it. Its quality can be controlled in the same ways that side light can be. In the photograph at right, the light source has been diffused with a sheet of translucent sailcloth; commercial diffusion film would have worked as well. Notice the soft shadow directly beneath the wooden bowl. The background is grey Formica bent into a gentle curve, and the light source has been carefully baffled to create a gradual dropping off of light toward the upper portions of the background.

In the Egyptian head, top right, a single, undiffused light was used. The light color of the piece serves as a natural "fill," keeping the resulting shadows from being too dark, and probably wouldn't work as well with a darker piece. This treatment even suggests the bright, direct sun of the work's origin.

Courtesy Boston Museum of Fine Arts.

Gary Gilman

Most of the principles and techniques illustrated on these pages are just as applicable to three-dimensional work as to flat work, but for reasons of space and clarity have been primarily shown in terms of their effects on two-dimensional work. The photographs illustrating three-dimensional lighting technique, however, are only pertinent to three-dimensional work.

**Shooting Work Under Glass.** If at all possible, remove an artwork from its frame to photograph it. But if you must shoot it under glass, you should baffle the camera to keep it from being reflected in the glass, as described in chapter 3. Dark artwork is likely to present the biggest reflection problem, because it combines with the glass to act as a mirror, as in the photograph at bottom left. In the photograph at top left, a sheet of black poster board with a hole cut in it for the lens has blocked out the reflection of photographer and copy stand.

**Matching the film for the light.**
These pictures show the effect of shooting film of the wrong color balance for the light being used. The yellow-orange rendition, top, illustrates the common mistake of using daylight-balanced film in tungsten light. The blue cast in the version at center shows the effect of shooting tungsten-balanced film in daylight. (Shooting daylight film by blue skylight, such as in open shade or by a window, will also produce a blue result, although usually less extreme than this.) The photograph with correct color, bottom, was produced by shooting Type B film (Ektachrome) in the 3200 degrees Kelvin light it is balanced for. An 81A filter was used to reduce the risk of bluish highlights.

**Matching the correct lamp with tungsten film.** As explained in chapter 2, tungsten films and the lamps made for them are actually designed for two different color temperatures of light, rated 3200 degrees and 3400 degrees on the Kelvin scale. These pictures show the effect of mismatching the two. The top photograph illustrates the effect of shooting Type A film (Kodachrome KPA), which is balanced for 3400-degree light, in 3200-degree light. The center photograph shows the effect of shooting Type B film (Ektachrome) which is balanced for 3200-degree light, in 3400-degree light. The photograph with correct color, at bottom, shows the effect of shooting Type B film in 3200-degree light, or Type A film in 3400-degree light.

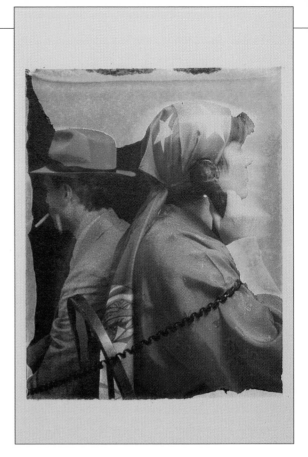

## Effect of fluorescent light.

These three pictures show the effect of fluorescent light on color rendition. The top left photograph was made on tungsten-balanced (Type B Ektachrome) film, which "sees" fluorescent light as extremely blue. Daylight film, top right, yields better color, but records a greenish cast. When this cast is eliminated by shooting through a CC 30 Magenta filter, bottom right, the color recorded by daylight film in cool white fluorescent light is fairly accurate, but the diffuse quality of the light tends to reduce image contrast.

Celie Fago

**Effect of "Pushing" Film.** As explained in chapter 7, "pushing" film involves setting a higher ISO than that recommended for the film, then having the color lab compensate for the resulting underexposure of the film by developing it longer. This technique will allow you to use smaller lens apertures or faster shutter speeds than the light would otherwise require, but it is also useful in increasing the contrast of an artwork with close values, whether light or dark. The top slide was exposed at the recommended ISO for the film (50) and processed normally. The bottom slide was exposed at double the recommended ISO (100) and pushed one stop. This technique has its trade-offs; here it has improved the sense of texture, but caused the colors to change slightly. Keep in mind that push-processing is best done with E-6 process films such as the Ektachromes.

Fujichrome 50.

Ralph Helmick

Ektachrome 64.

Kodachrome 64.

Ektachrome
with 81B filter.

Kodachrome
with 81B filter.

**Color and Outdoor Installation Views.** The color rendition of different daylight-balanced slide films varies quite a bit, as shown in the pictures on the left, all taken in the same light. The photographs on the right, above, show the effect of using an 81B warming filter with the Ektachrome, top, and Kodachrome, bottom. This filter is useful for shooting color film outdoors on an overcast day, because it eliminates the bluish cast the film usually records.

No filter.

Pina

**Effect of Warming Filters in Tungsten Light.** This series shows the effect of 81 series filters on color rendition. The top left photograph was taken on Kodachrome KPA in 3400-degree light, without filtration. The bottom left photograph was taken with the same combination of light and film, using an 81 filter on the lens; top right, with an 81A filter; and bottom right, with an 81B filter. Notice how the blues are weakened and warm colors enriched with stronger filtration. For this image, which has both sides of the spectrum, an 81 or 81A seems the best choice.

81 filter.

81A filter.

81B filter.

**Importance of Details.** The people who review slides of your work often don't project them. For this reason, if your work is difficult to "read" when it's reduced to the tiny area of the 35mm slide, you should supply them with details of it as well. In two-dimensional work, this may give a sense of detail or texture that an overall view can't provide; in three-dimensional work, as here, it can give a sense of structure and articulation in a piece that may appear to lack them in the overall view.

Hope Ricciardi

Jon Neprud

**Exposure for Dark Artwork.**
Whether two- or three-dimensional, an artwork composed primarily of dark values may require exposure above and beyond that indicated by the gray card. The top photograph was given the exposure indicated by the gray card; the center photograph, one-half stop of extra exposure. The bottom photograph, which was given a full stop of additional exposure, shows the surfaces and colors of the artwork most clearly. When in doubt, bracket your exposure for a dark work in half-stop increments up to one and a half stops *over* the indicated exposure.

Diefo

One stop
underexposed.

One-half stop
underexposed.

Slide exposed for
gray card reading.

One-half stop
overexposed.

One stop
overexposed.

**Importance of Bracketing Exposures.** These photographs show the effect of bracketing in half-stop increments on both the "over" and "under" side of the exposure indicated by your gray card reading. Sometimes this will produce at least two acceptable exposures, as here, where both the gray card exposure and the one-half stop "under" exposure are acceptable. Notice the loss of color in the overexposed slides. *Always* bracket your exposures.

Susan Morrison

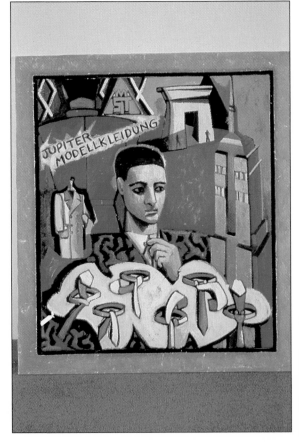

**Effect of Slide Duplication.** Although a good color lab can, through careful technique, make a duplicate slide that is very close to the original, a dupe will usually display subtle color changes and an increase in contrast. If the original slide seems flat, the increase in contrast can actually make the dupe look better than the original, but more often than not the changes will be undesirable. Here, the top left photograph is from the original slide; the top right photograph, from a duplicate of the original; and the bottom right photograph, from a duplicate of the duplicate slide. Notice the increase in the intensity of the colors in the dupes; also notice how each generation crops out more of the original. In general, try to avoid duping slides; make as many originals as you think you will need.

Susan Mampre

## Color-Corrected Duplicate Slides.
For an additional charge, a professional lab will make a duplicate slide in which it adjusts the color of the original. The top photograph was shot with daylight-balanced slide film in a mixture of daylight and tungsten light. The tungsten component of the light caused a yellow cast in the original slide. The color lab added blue to the light used to make the corrected duplicate, bottom, restoring the neutral white of the wall. A good lab can also make a duplicate in which part of the original is enlarged to fill the frame, a correction which may be useful if you were far away from your artwork when you photographed it.

# APPENDIX **USEFUL ACCESSORIES**

The bare essentials that you will need to take good photographs of your artwork are discussed early in the book. They include a 35mm camera, a tripod, clip-on light fixtures, color-rated photoflood lamps, metal reflectors if you're not using reflector-style bulbs, and a photographic gray card. Other supplies that are almost as indispensable are a cable release, a warming filter (81A), and, of course, background and diffusion materials for three-dimensional work.

However, there are still other items—some as basic and inexpensive as masking tape—that may make the task of photographing your work easier. Some of them you will find around your home; others you will have to purchase, but do so only if you feel they can help you do a better job. These items are listed below, along with some of their uses. They are followed by a short list of mail-order suppliers of this sort of hardware.

**Baffling and reflecting materials.** Black matboard, poster board or construction paper, or black cloth, can be used to eliminate reflections in glassed or shiny work, or to block off light that might otherwise fall across the camera lens' front element. Also to cover surfaces adjacent to the work that might contribute a color cast to it. White matboard, poster board or heavy paper, or white cloth, can be used to create reflections in shiny work.

**Black foil.** A heavy, flexible matte-black aluminum sheeting, usually sold in small rolls by mail-order outfits. Because it is heat-resistant, it's particularly useful in controlling lighting effects. (It can, for example, be used to fashion a "snoot" around a metal reflector if you want a beam of light.)

**Black photographic tape.** An opaque tape available at well-stocked photography stores. Rather expensive, but especially good for securing baffling cards to your camera or lens when shooting work under glass, because it doesn't reflect. Also good for stopping light leaks.

**Bubble level or angle finder.** Useful in shooting flat artwork that is leaning against a wall; matching the camera's tilt to the artwork's simplifies squaring up.

**Clamps and clothespins.** Although gaffer tape will often suffice, clamps are often the most positive way to secure lighting paraphernalia. They come in a huge variety of designs and price. Clothespins can be clipped to wooden dowels to hold lightweight baffling and reflecting materials.

**Copy stand.** Described in detail in the box on page 51, the copy stand is a useful and time-saving alternative to the tripod for shooting small-to-medium size flat artwork, or smaller three-dimensional artwork (such as jewelry or ceramics) that you plan to "shoot down" on.

**Extension cords.** Make sure they're in good condition and that they are designed to withstand a 500- or 1000-watt load.

**Gaffer tape or duct tape.** A heavy-duty, very sticky gray tape useful for securing lighting hardware when you don't want to invest in fancy clamps.

**Masking tape.** Good for securing lightweight work on a wall, marking the location of tripod legs (or light stands) on the floor for future reference, or making register marks for speedier photography of more than one work.

**Photographic light stands.** Although you can clip your lighting fixtures to ladders, chair backs, and the like, these collapsible metal stands make adjusting the height and position of your lamps much easier. The sleeve-like coupling on some clip-on fixtures is designed to fit over the stand's uppermost rod. Expect to pay twenty dollars apiece for lightweight stands.

**Photographic umbrella.** Useful for softening light when photographing three-dimensional work, and described in more detail in that section. Bulbs are aimed into the umbrella, and the light from them is bounced back at the artwork in a much more diffuse form. Silver-lined umbrellas are more efficient reflectors. (Flat panels with high efficiency for bounce lighting are also available.) This kind of paraphernalia is easier to use with mounting hardware for a light stand.

**Supplementary close-up lenses.** Simple positive lenses in filter-type mounts, which screw into the front thread of your lens to increase its close-focusing range. Usually sold in sets, but the weakest—labeled " +1"—will often do the trick by itself.

**Tape measure.** Can be handy for positioning camera and lights symmetrically, which makes lighting two-dimensional work much faster and easier.

## SUPPLIERS

List of mail-order suppliers of photographic and lighting hardware and software:

Calumet Photographic, Inc.
890 Supreme Drive
Bensenville, IL 60106

Porter's Camera Store, Inc.
Post Office Box 628
Cedar Falls, Iowa 50613

Spiratone Inc.
135-06 Northern Blvd.
Flushing, NY 11354

# INDEX

## ABOUT THE AUTHOR

Russell Hart, author/reviser of *The New Joy of Photography,* is currently senior editor of *Popular Photography.* He has also served as a contributing editor to Petersen's *PhotoGraphic* magazine; freelanced as an editorial photographer for the Polaroid Corporation and *Boston* magazine; taught photography at Tufts University, Mount Ida College, and the School at the Museum of Fine Arts in Boston; and has acted as a consultant to the Boston Museum's photography department. As an exhibiting artist, he also has extensive firsthand experience with the slide-submission aspect of *Photographing Your Artwork.*

# Other Art Books from North Light

**Graphics/Business of Art**

**Airbrushing the Human Form**, by Andy Charlesworth $27.95 (cloth)
**Artist's Friendly Legal Guide**, by Conner, Karlen, Perwin & Spatt $15.95 (paper)
**Artist's Market: Where & How to Sell Your Graphic Art, (Annual Directory)** $18.95 (cloth)
**Basic Graphic Design & Paste-Up**, by Jack Warren $12.95 (paper)
**Color Harmony: A Guide to Creative Color Combinations**, by Hideaki Chijiiwa $15.95 (paper)
**Complete Airbrush & Photoretouching Manual**, by Peter Owen & John Sutcliffe $23.95 (cloth)
**The Complete Guide to Greeting Card Design & Illustration**, by Eva Szela $27.95 (cloth)
**Creating Dynamic Roughs**, by Alan Swann $27.95 (cloth)
**Creative Ad Design & Illustration**, by Dick Ward $32.95 (cloth)
**Creative Director's Sourcebook**, by Nick Souter & Stuart Newman $89.00 (cloth)
**Design Rendering Techniques**, by Dick Powell $29.95 (cloth)
**Dynamic Airbrush**, by David Miller & James Effler $29.95 (cloth)
**Getting It Printed**, by Beach, Shepro & Russon $29.50 (paper)
**The Graphic Artist's Guide to Marketing & Self Promotion**, by Sally Prince Davis $15.95 (paper)
**Handbook of Pricing & Ethical Guidelines**, 6th edition, by The Graphic Artist's Guild $19.95 (paper)
**How to Design Trademarks & Logos**, by Murphy & Rowe $24.95 (cloth)
**How to Draw & Sell Comic Strips**, by Alan McKenzie $18.95 (cloth)
**How to Understand & Use Design & Layout**, by Alan Swann $24.95 (cloth)
**How to Understand & Use Grids**, by Alan Swann $27.95
**Living by Your Brush Alone**, by Edna Wagner Piersol $16.95 (paper)
**Marker Rendering Techniques**, by Dick Powell & Patricia Monahan $32.95 (cloth)
**Papers for Printing**, by Mark Beach & Ken Russon $34.50 (paper)
**Presentation Techniques for the Graphic Artist**, by Jenny Mulherin $24.95 (cloth)
**Ready to Use Layouts for Desktop Design**, by Chris Prior $27.95 (cloth)
**Sir William Russell Flint**, by Ralph Lewis and Keith Gardner $55.00 (cloth)
**Studio Secrets for the Graphic Artist**, by Jack Buchan $29.95 (cloth)
**Type: Design, Color, Character & Use**, by Michael Beaumont $24.95 (cloth)

**Watercolor**

**Getting Started in Watercolor**, by John Blockley $19.95 (paper)
**The New Spirit of Watercolor**, by Mike Ward $27.95 (cloth)
**Painting Nature's Details in Watercolor**, by Cathy Johnson $24.95 (cloth)
**Painting Watercolor Portraits That Glow**, by Jan Kunz $27.95 (cloth)
**Starting with Watercolor**, by Rowland Hilder $24.95 (cloth)
**Watercolor Painter's Solution Book**, by Angela Gair $24.95 (cloth)
**Watercolor—The Creative Experience**, by Barbara Nechis $16.95 (paper)
**Watercolor Tricks & Techniques**, by Cathy Johnson $24.95 (cloth)
**Watercolor Workbook**, by Bud Biggs & Lois Marshall $19.95 (paper)
**Watercolor: You Can Do It!**, by Tony Couch $25.95 (cloth)

**Mixed Media**

**Catching Light in Your Paintings**, by Charles Sovek $18.95 (paper)
**Colored Pencil Drawing Techniques**, by Iain Hutton-Jamieson $23.95 (cloth)
**The Complete Oil Painting Book**, by Wendon Blake $29.95 (cloth)
**Exploring Color**, by Nita Leland $26.95 (cloth)
**Keys to Drawing**, by Bert Dodson $21.95 (cloth)
**The North Light Illustrated Book of Painting Techniques**, by Elizabeth Tate $27.95 (cloth)
**Oil Painting: A Direct Approach**, by Joyce Pike $26.95 (cloth)
**Pastel Painting Techniques**, by Guy Roddon $24.95 (cloth)
**The Pencil**, by Paul Calle $16.95 (paper)
**People Painting Scrapbook**, by J. Everett Draper $26.95 (cloth)

To order directly from the publisher, include $2.50 postage and handling for one book, 50¢ for each additional book. Allow 30 days for delivery.

**North Light Books**
**1507 Dana Avenue, Cincinnati, Ohio 45207**
Credit card orders call TOLL-FREE
1-800-543-4644 (Outside Ohio)
1-800-551-0884 (Ohio only)
Prices subject to change without notice.